"Food can be a most effective agent of change. F .... be it's another pair of shears to clear the baby trail. Armed with the energizing, tasty treats of The Fertile Kitchen™ Cookbook, you might hike up that trail with more ease and an extra bounce in your step."

– Julia Indichova, author of The Fertile Female and Inconceivable, founder of www.fertileheart.com

"When trying to conceive, changing my diet was one of the most effective fertility treatments I found. Figuring out a strict fertility diet was tough going on my own. This cookbook gives great, straightforward guidance on making a healthy fertility diet part of your life. My husband and I have tried some of the recipes, and not only do they taste great, but even my non-chef husband can easily follow the step-by-step pictures and instructions."

– Alison Armstrong, Designer and Mom to 4-year-old daughter

"If I was trying to stick to a specific plan for diet/health/fertility concerns, I would definitely buy this book. ...The dishes we made [from this cookbook] were easy, yummy, and required only a quick clean up. I also liked that most of the "extra" ingredients we needed (garlic, oil, salt, pepper, dill and so on) were "normal" items we had already stocked in our kitchen."

– Karen Kelly, Co-founder and CEO of a market research company

"I just finished testing a handful of recipes. I was surprised how flavorful they were considering the minimal amount of seasonings used—and all were so easy to make. I would buy this book just for the healthful recipe selections alone."

– Vené Franco, Freelance Food Writer and Editor

"I must say that in addition to the recipes tasting great, Pierre Giauque's sense of seasoning is right on! I usually have to adjust the salt and pepper in most recipes, but the amounts in the recipes I tried enhanced without overpowering the other flavors."

– Louisa Verma, Researcher

Cover photograph Copyright © 2009 by Frank Richardson

All photographs within the book Copyright © 2009 by Cindy Bailey

Author photograph of Pierre Giauque Copyright © 2009 by Frank Richardson

Author photograph of Cindy Bailey Copyright © 2009 by Antonia Kao

Cover and book design by Erin Pace

Fertile Kitchen is a trademark of Cindy Bailey and Pierre Giauque

Library of Congress Control Number: 2009908011

ISBN: 978-0-578-03480-5

THE Fertile Kitchen™
COOKBOOK

Simple Recipes for Optimizing Your Fertility

For our son Julien, who, against the odds, is here,
filling our days with endless joy.

For Lucie Giauque, ma petite Maman chérie.

For the beautiful women and men
traveling this life-changing road to meet their child.

Table of Contents

Acknowledgements V

Foreword VII

Introduction 1

About this Book 5

The Fertile Kitchen™ Dietary Guidelines 9

    Tips for Following the Dietary Guidelines 10

    Dietary Guidelines 11

    Lifestyle Factors.. 25

    Quick Guide to Fertile Kitchen™ Dietary Guidelines 28

Getting Ready to Cook... 29

    Cooking Basics... 29

        Preparing to Cook 29

        Useful Cooking Tips 30

        Equipment to Use 31

        Common Cooking Terms 33

        Food Quantities Table 35

        Conversion Tables 36

    Ingredients: What to Buy and Where to Find It 38

    Substitutions and Creativity... 40

    Spices 41

The Fertile Kitchen™ Recipes.. 45

    Breakfast 47

        Spinach and Mushroom Omelet 48

        Blueberry Pancakes 50

        Eggs in Different Styles 52

        Oatmeal.. 54

Rice and Grains 57
  Garlic Pasta 58
  Fried Rice 60
  Fluffy Rice 62
  Pasta with Olives and Pine Nuts 64
  Light Mushroom Risotto 66
  Zucchini Pasta 68
  Pizza a la Polenta 70
  Mixed Rice and Vegetables 72
  Crêpes Salées 74

Vegetables 77
  Sautéed Leeks 78
  Sautéed Mushrooms in Lemon Juice 80
  Mixed Vegetables 82
  Roasted Baby Bell Peppers 84
  Stuffed Vegetables 86
  Steamed Vegetables 88
  Schezwan Green Beans 90
  Sautéed Spinach 92
  Sautéed Fennel 94
  Sautéed Bok Choy 96
  Carrots with Garlic and Cilantro 98
  BBQ Marinated Asparagus 100

Beans and Other Legumes 103
  Chili con Carne 104
  Lentils with Onions 106
  Spicy Garbanzo Beans 108
  Black Beans 110

Meat and Poultry 113
  Chicken in Tomato Sauce 114
  Lamb Stew 116
  Lamb Roast 118
  Lamb Curry in Coconut Milk 120

Ground Turkey Mix 122

Chicken and Broccoli Rice Noodles 124

Chicken en Papillotes 126

Chicken with Bell Peppers and Mushrooms 128

Chicken with Portobello Mushrooms 130

Seafood 133

Hot and Spicy Prawns 134

Garlic Prawns 136

Steamed Fish Filet and Vegetables 138

Baked Salmon Filet 140

Baked Fish 142

Seafood Soup 144

Soups and Salads 147

Broccoli Soup 148

Rice Salad 150

Hearty Tomato Soup 152

Pasta Salad 154

Vietnamese Chicken Noodle Soup 156

Lentil Soup 158

Sides and Sauces 161

Hummus 162

Guacamole 164

Mushroom Sauce 166

Healthy Béchamel Sauce 168

Pierre's Vinaigrette Salad Dressing 170

Desserts 173

Juicy Fruit Salad 174

Crêpes Sucrées 176

Index 179

Acknowledgements

A book such as this does not get made by the hands (and minds) of its authors alone. Many contribute to its success. On our journey to share these wonderful recipes and information, we relied on many for their generous advice, support, encouragement and contributions.

We first and foremost would like to thank Philip E. Chenette, M.D., of Pacific Fertility Center, for contributing the beautiful Foreword to our book. We are also grateful for his general support, and for his own interest in nutrition and commitment to helping couples overcome obstacles to parenthood.

We would also like to thank Julia Indichova, author of *The Fertile Female* and founder of the FertileHeart™ community, for her support. She is the "real deal," and her dedication to helping women with fertility issues is a great inspiration to us.

A deep thank you to our dear friends, Karen and Bill Kelly, who from the beginning, tirelessly answered questions and fed us brilliant ideas. We would also like to thank food writer extraordinaire, Vené Franco, for her constant support and advice, also from the start of this project.

Thank you to so many others who answered questions or gave advice, support and/or feedback on early versions of this book, including: Jennifer Basye Sander, Dawn Yun, Dianne Jacob, Virginia Watkins, Michel Giauque, Chris Bailey, Jennifer Gunter, Callie Kindrish, Kathy Brozek, Gloria Saltzman, Edy Greenblatt, Claude Laviano, Michele Niesen, Antonia Kao, Renée Frisbie, Molly Muro, Katrina Norwood and Scott James (aka Kemble Scott).

We are grateful to Frank Richardson for his gorgeous cover photograph, and to our neighbors Rhonda and Gene Scattini for use of their fabulous kitchen. A huge thank you also goes to Erin Pace for her beautiful, sleek design of this book, inside and out.

Thanks to all who tested our recipes too: Alison Armstrong, Vené Franco, Karen Kelly, Lara Walters, Tia Sommer, Jayne Frigon, Craig Bannatyne, Dan and Mary Madoni, and Louisa Verma.

Cindy would also like to thank her writing groups, whose members fill her with awe and inspiration every time: the Writing Mamas (led by Dawn Yun) and Writers Who Wine (led by Jennifer Basye Sander).

Last but absolutely not least, we would like to thank our dynamic, enthusiastic, "can-do" publishing team: Michelle Gamble-Risley and Michele Smith of 3L Publishing for believing in our book and helping us to make it real!

Foreword

The biological imperative to reproduce can feel so strong, emotional and urgent that men and women feel a sense of overwhelming frustration, sadness and depression when it doesn't happen. About 7.3 million couples in the U.S. alone experience some kind of challenge when it comes to conception and pregnancy. What should come naturally to one couple may turn into a medical event for another. The pain, sadness and frustration a couple experiences can even wreak enough havoc on a once strong relationship to cause its dissolution.

For all those that find conception so easy, the goal remains elusive for so many others. Barriers to conception can emerge from age, illness or genetic pre-disposition—and in some cases, barriers remain unknown. Conception can only occur once a month, and when conception fails, frustration and disappointment mount. Over time, these issues can become a stressful fertility problem.

For conception to occur, the environment must be just right. Each conception is a one in a trillion event. One egg of the millions that are present at birth, one sperm of the 100 million at each ejaculate, combine to produce an embryo. The odds against any one sperm or egg are astronomical. If fertilization is achieved—a difficult event in and of itself—the even more challenging processes of cell division and finding a healthy spot in the uterus to implant begin. Conditions must be precise for the embryo to develop.

It is rather stunning that reproduction happens as easily as it does so often. Reproduction is a highly complex process that is the result of millions of years of evolution, highly tuned genetic and physiologic processes, and a great deal of luck. The basics of reproduction—ovulation, ejaculation, delivery of the gametes to the female reproductive tract, fertilization, implantation, and early growth of the embryo—are well understood, but the process of reproduction is far more complex than these relatively simple technical details.

At fertilization, the embryo provides a recipe for its development. The genetic code recorded on the 23 pairs of chromosomes offers many possible pathways to create a child. For the individual cell, there are codes for making proteins, codes for the machinery that produces the proteins, and codes for the energy apparatus that supports the production of those proteins. There are codes for integrating the cells into the body—combining cells to create tissues and organs, codes for the senses, detection of light, heat, taste and smell, codes for the heart and plumbing, and codes for the brain and nervous system to run the whole apparatus. An amazingly complex recipe, but nothing more than an instruction set—and far from the finished product.

Producing a baby from this recipe is a different matter altogether. It has become quite clear that there are many ways of interpreting the recipe supplied by the embryo. A particular protein code may have a dozen different pathways of production. Pathway A may produce a healthy active protein, while pathways B, C and D may produce an abnormal protein with little functional utility.

Which pathway is chosen is the result of a complex interplay of the recipe with the *environment*. The surrounding fluids, energy, proteins, amino acids, vitamins, carbohydrates and fats that are available to the embryo determine the execution of the recipe. If some nutrient is in short supply, Pathway B may be taken over by Pathway A, resulting in loss of an essential protein. Interpretation of the recipe is highly dependent on the environment in which this happens, which in turn is dependent on diet.

Maintaining the correct conditions in that environment is the goal of nutrition. Reproduction will only occur when plentiful raw materials co-exist. Adequate levels of protein, carbohydrates and fats, and the raw materials of vitamins, minerals and energy sources are required for production of the gametes, preparation of the uterus, and maintenance of the early pregnancy.

Nutrition also plays a role in conception. In adults, low-fat diets increase the risk of ovulation disorders. Vitamin supplements reduce the risk. Sperm production is enhanced by nutritional supplements and decreased by nutritional insults like alcohol and poor diet.

Changes in maternal nutrition directly affect the risk of birth defects. Neural tube defects, such as spina bifida and anencephaly, are related to insufficient folic acid levels in the diet. Essential oils such as DHA and omega-3 are important for brain and eye development. Maternal diet is also known to affect future childhood performance in school.

Our science is only beginning to unravel these mysteries, but there is no doubt that every human is a product of a unique recipe in the form of DNA from the sperm and egg in combination with nutritional building blocks needed to interpret that recipe. A good recipe, with adequate building blocks, is essential to the outcome of a healthy child.

Where do these building blocks come from? The food we eat. Breakfast, lunch and dinner, the carbohydrates, oils and proteins that comprise our diets are processed into basic components of amino acids, sugars and fats that make up our cells. That's why nutrition in pre-conception is so important to embryonic development.

We know that altering the ratio of energy sources available in the first days of embryo development may dramatically influence early growth to the blastocyst stage, the stage at which the embryo is ready to attach to the uterine wall. Missing raw materials, such as amino acids and essential oils, may result in failure of the placenta and errors in brain and eye formation. Diet also appears to have some influence on gender development too.

Improving diet is essential to achieving the goal of a healthy child. Good genes, a healthy reproductive apparatus, and all the raw materials that nutrition provides must be in place. I am so pleased to see this renewed emphasis on diet and fertility, and look forward to using *The Fertile Kitchen*™ in my own practice.

Philip E. Chenette, M.D.
Medical Director
Pacific Fertility Center
www.pacificfertilitycenter.com

Introduction

Cindy writes:

At age 40, after trying to get pregnant with my husband for over a year, I visited a popular reproductive endocrinologist (a fertility doctor) in Northern California who gave me the hard news: that I had a two percent chance of conceiving on my own.

In that moment, my heart turned to lead and dropped to the floor. I had already heard the hysteria about how difficult it can be to get pregnant in one's forties, and I knew my follicle stimulating hormone (FSH) had started to rise—indicating that my stash of eggs was losing quality and/or quantity, but two percent? That number alone put me into panic. It said to me, "Forget it, it's impossible, you will never be a mother." I wanted to scream!

In my frustration, panic and deep sadness, I was not alone. A Harvard study revealed that women who want a child and are told they can't have one react with the same level of depression and stress as those who are told they have cancer or AIDS. The sense of loss is profound.

In the doctor's office that day, however, I also had another reaction. I simply, flat out refused to accept the doctor's grim prognosis. "Where do these statistics come from anyway?" I wondered. "Who are these other people lumped into the two percent with me?" I decided right then and there I was not a statistic. I was an individual, and I could make a difference in my own fertility. I had already begun researching natural, holistic methods of aiding fertility, and I knew in my gut this was true.

I had another motivation for this attitude: It was simply and utterly *unacceptable* to me that I don't get to have a child. I refused to believe that. My mind wouldn't even let the idea in. I had a strong sense that my future child was out there, waiting for me to be ready, and I was not about to let him or her down by giving up. I made a commitment to do everything in my power to meet this child.

Of course, the odds were against me, but that was no excuse not to challenge them. I had nothing to lose and everything to gain. Creating a baby was the most important ambition in my life. Instead of statistics—which I completely blocked from my mind—I chose to believe in *possibility*. Possibility is an open invitation, there to explore if we choose, and I for one did not want to have any regrets for not exploring this possibility to the fullest.

A month before walking into the doctor's office that day, I had already begun to make changes. Bolstered by research, I put myself on a strict fertility friendly diet, among other natural healing regimens, such as yoga, visualizations, meditation and supplements.

Four months later, to the astonishment of my doctor and to my own breathless amazement, I got pregnant naturally and later delivered a healthy baby (our son, Julien).

That experience taught me a lot about trusting my instincts and my body, believing in myself in spite of the odds, and accepting that I had the power to make a difference.

We all have that power—much more of it than we think, or allow ourselves to believe.

It's true that in the end, it's not only up to us. Conception holds an element of wondrous mystery, and over that mystery we have little control. We can meet it halfway, though, because we do have control over our bodies, minds and emotions—even if it doesn't feel like it sometimes—and we can bring them all into focus with the goal of having a baby. We only have to choose to do it.

Changing my diet to aid conception was actually the second time I had used food as part of a regimen to resolve an "impossible" condition. Years before, I used nutritional healing to cure me of a mysterious illness I had for several months and for which well-respected doctors could not identify or treat. Three months into a self-imposed dietary regimen, all my symptoms lifted. The fact that it actually worked truly amazed me!

And here it was, working again!

Diet Makes a Difference

I believe deeply and passionately that what we eat makes a difference in our health. That makes sense, doesn't it? If diet can play a key role in helping us fight certain conditions, such as diabetes, heart disease or cancer, why can't it be used to aid reproduction? Well, it can, and many others—from mainstream doctors to alternative healthcare practitioners—agree. You can just Google "fertility diet" on the Internet to see.

Following a fertility diet, as I learned, is hard work—especially when it comes on top of so much other hard work and sacrifices we women with fertility issues make to meet our dream of motherhood. Its restrictions mean having to eat in every day, and I for one loved eating out. I didn't like cooking.

Easing the Process

What eased the process for me was not only the impressive degree of support from my husband and co-author, Pierre Giauque, but his cooking. He took it as a personal challenge to create a variety of dishes within the strict dietary requirements to support our efforts toward becoming parents.

Specifically, he asked himself, "How can I take this restrictive list of foods and still turn out original, savory dishes? How can I produce enough variety so that we never get bored and give up? And how can I keep all that cooking easy and manageable on top of so many other life demands, especially considering that, by the nature of the diet, we'll be shopping for sometimes hard-to-find produce and products and having to eat at home all the time?"

The result is the 60 or so flexible, easy-to-make recipes presented in this cookbook. Amazingly, you won't even notice these dishes have no sugar, dairy or wheat! And that's the point. Pierre also included information to make every step of the cooking process so straightforward that even a "kitchen klutz" like me could do it.

Not only did Pierre's recipes make it much easier to stick to the diet, but they also helped us reconnect as a couple during a very difficult and stressful time. Preparing, cooking and eating these meals kept us focused on a positive project toward parenthood that we could do together, and our relationship strengthened as a result.

Naturally, we wanted to share these recipes—along with our dietary insights gained through years of research and consulting with leaders in the field—in hopes that it could ease the burden on other couples struggling to become parents, just as it had eased ours. We wanted women, in particular, to feel as I did—healthy and empowered by this process.

In the end, I found it amazing what can happen when you feed your body what it needs to heal, you believe in yourself, and you surrender to possibility.

If eating this way worked for me, I believe it can work for you too. Of course, there is no guarantee that following any diet is going to get you pregnant; everyone is different. The worst case scenario is that you put your body in the healthiest, best possible position for conception—and that alone is a really good thing.

Here are some general tips that I found helpful on my journey:

1. Believe in yourself without doubt. See the end in mind and don't let go. Your future child needs you to believe in him or her.

2. Do all you can. You have more power than you think.

3. Nurture yourself along the way, give yourself breaks.

4. Surrender. This might be the hardest step of all. After you've done all you can, you need to let go and allow the mystery to unfold.

A Little About the Recipes

Pierre writes:

As Cindy mentioned, I developed the recipes in this cookbook as a challenge and to support our efforts to conceive. My aim was to create a full spectrum of easy-to-make dishes that together embody variety and flavor despite the dietary restrictions. You'll find that here, along with ethnically diverse dishes that evolved from my upbringing and travels.

Born and raised in Lausanne, Switzerland, my first forays into cooking were naturally French-inspired. However, through later travels, my cooking became infused with the flavors and styles of Italy, Spain, Portugal, eastern Africa, India, the U.S. and other places. As a result, you'll even find recipes here that are hybrids of multiple culinary cultures—all healthy and delicious.

Some of my signature dishes included here are *Lamb Curry in Coconut Milk*, *Crêpes Salée*, *Spicy Garbanzo Beans*, *Ground Turkey Mix* and a light version of *Chili Con Carne*. These are also favorites among friends and family.

Our hope is that in making these recipes, you'll experience a new adventure for cooking, enjoy the healthy, flavorful food, and not really notice too much that you're even on a diet. Even better, we hope that eating healthy like this becomes a habit for life.

About this Book

By design, this cookbook is intended to be an easy-to-use tool to support you on your journey toward parenthood. Here's how:

- In its layout, full color presentation and simple-to-follow recipes, this cookbook makes rigid dietary guidelines easy to take. Information is effortless to find, and guidelines and recipes, painless to follow.

- Recipes are practical, not sophisticated. They are straightforward, yet full of flavor, variety and ethnic diversity so you won't get bored and give up.

- We made our recipes flexible so that you can effortlessly accommodate substitutions for a less strict diet, or to meet your own dietary preferences or needs.

- We include expert advice. We base recipes on generally accepted dietary guidelines, those which represent current prevalent dietary wisdom in the area of fertility, and are backed by research and common sense. It's also the diet that worked for us.

- We wrote dietary guidelines so they're simple to follow. We also wrote this book as a supplement to your efforts to conceive; however, it is intentionally not a medical book filled with scientific analysis. We kept it simple: just stating what you can and cannot eat (or do) and why.

- Our cookbook provides it all in one place—everything you need to succeed on this diet, including what foods to buy and eat, and where to find them; basic equipment needed; cooking basics and more. If you have never followed a diet as strict as this one before or are new to cooking, we have a section for you!

- We understand what busy lives we all lead on top of the drain of fertility issues and we provide shortcut options to save on effort or time—such as accommodating the use of organic canned tomatoes instead of fresh ones, if it's easier or necessary.

Although our dietary guidelines and tips are backed by research and represent what worked for us, we encourage you to choose for yourself what makes sense to you on this journey. Everyone is different and has unique needs. Our recipes are flexible to accommodate changes if required.

Who this Book Is for

This cookbook is for:

- Women and couples who are having trouble conceiving—that is, they have been trying to conceive for six months or more without success—whether or not they seek medical assistance.

  Even if medical procedures are required to aid conception, as in the case of blocked tubes, for example, optimal nutrition may still improve success of those procedures. Check with a reproductive endocrinologist (a fertility specialist) to learn more.

- Men who wish to support their partners in a cooking project they can share together as well as men with fertility issues themselves.

  We also recommend that men go on the diet even if they have no known fertility issues themselves. Ten to 15 percent of couples have unexplained infertility and you can never know for sure how much of a couple's total fertility comes from that.

- Anyone interested in a healthier, cleaner diet for long-term health.

- Cooks and non-cooks alike, as this cookbook supports new cooks.

How to Use this Book

This is how we recommend you use this book:

- Review dietary guidelines to know what and how to eat. If you're only eating from our recipes, you don't have to memorize a thing! It is useful to know what to eat when you're not, however, or if you need to make substitutions.

- Review the *Getting Ready to Cook* chapter based on your needs. This section includes information and tips on what to buy, such as organic produce and wheat-free alternatives, and where to find them.

- Use the table of contents or index to decide which recipes you'd like to make.

- Follow the recipes. All recipes use the same consistent format for ease of use, with full color photos of the finished product, ingredients and selected stages of preparation.

- To make substitutions and additions based on your own personal nutritional needs or preferences, see the *Substitutions and Creativity* section of the *Getting Ready to Cook* chapter.

The Fertile Kitchen™ Dietary Guidelines

Cindy writes:

Of all the systems in the body (digestive, immune, respiratory and so on), the reproductive system is the most expendable. You don't need it to survive. So when the body is stressed, it's one of the first systems to be neglected or shut down. The body redirects energy elsewhere. This is why reducing stress is so important when trying to conceive.

Stress comes in many forms, though. Eating the wrong foods also stresses the body. Alcohol, for example, taxes your liver. Processed sugar not only creates a spike in blood sugar levels, but can also strain your immune system, negatively impacting fertility. You definitely don't want that!

What you want instead is to reduce stress on the body in order to make more energy available to support your endocrine function (which regulates hormones) and general reproductive system. Also, because digestion requires more labor than any other process in the body, another important goal is to ease the energy expended by digestion so that, once again, you have more for reproduction. At the same time, you want to provide fertility-boosting, healthy nutrients to your body.

By eating this way—to support your body and its hormonal health—you optimize chances of conception and help create a nourishing, welcoming place to receive a baby.

The dietary guidelines we present in this chapter support these goals. We based our principles on common dietary wisdom gleaned from both mainstream and alternative healthcare practioners—and backed our theories with research. This is also the diet that helped us conceive and bring home our own healthy baby.

In a nutshell, these guidelines mean you need to:

- Get rid of foods that have a negative impact on the body, such as alcohol, caffeine and processed sugar.

- Keep or add foods that benefit, nourish and heal, such as vegetables, beans and whole grains.

- Eat foods closer to your body temperature (warm), so as not to overly tax your digestion to heat (or cool) foods. For the same reason, you also need to avoid overly spicy foods and cold beverages. Note that our guidelines make an exception for occasional salads.

- Avoid hard-to-digest foods, such as dairy products.

- Avoid raw meat and fish, which can harbor bacteria.

- Go for as much variety as possible for the highest nutritional value.

- Consider the balance that comes from eating a variety of foods in combination and overall. For example, one food may cause a more rapid rise in blood sugar (something we don't want), but eaten in combination with foods that do not will mellow this effect.

By following these dietary guidelines as a whole you automatically avoid most refined carbohydrates, keep your blood sugar stabilized overall, maximize nutritional value, and contribute to a general healthy balance.

Tips for Following the Dietary Guidelines

Eating is as much a habit as it is an essential function, and changing habits can be hard work, which is the main reason we created this cookbook—to ease the process with simple, yet flavorful recipes. Some additional recommendations to keep in mind include the following.

- Although our guidelines are backed by research, it is important to follow only what makes sense to you. Everyone is different and has unique needs. Our flexible recipes easily allow for substitutions.

- Ease into the diet, eliminating one to three items at a time over the course of a few weeks. It can be daunting to go cold turkey.

- Give the diet time. It initially takes two to three weeks for old cravings to subside and the body to cleanse. Stick to the diet closely during this time, although you should do so afterwards, as well. Afterwards, give yourself about three months before your body fully responds to the changes.

- Diet doesn't work alone. Get plenty of rest and reduce stress. For additional tips, see the *Lifestyle Factors* section at the end of this chapter.

- Do not use this diet to lose weight! This is not the time for that. Your body needs nourishment, abundance and healing right now. Don't let yourself go hungry, either, which stresses the body. On this diet, you should feel satisfied and fulfilled. Keep in mind that fat is important for fertility. If you believe you are overweight, see the section, *Maintain a Healthy Body Mass Index*.

Dietary Guidelines

These guidelines provide information on the reasons behind the food choices, their relevance to fertility and helpful tips. To make them easier to follow and to aid while shopping or at a restaurant, we also provide an easy-to-use *Quick Guide* on p.28.

No Alcohol

I know how nice a glass of wine at the end of the day or at a social gathering can be to unwind and de-stress, but if you're going for a baby, you *have* to find a more body friendly way to cope. No exceptions. Alcohol needs to be eliminated.

To your body, alcohol is a toxin. Not only does it disrupt the absorption of nutrients, create more work for your body (and liver), and weaken your immune system, but it also raises prolactin levels, which can interfere with ovulation. (Prolactin is the hormone that stimulates breast milk and inhibits ovulation.)

One study showed that even as little as one alcoholic drink a week can dramatically reduce a couple's odds of conceiving. Enough said.

Men should at least avoid alcohol. Excessive use may result in a rise in estrogen levels, which can interfere with sperm development and hormone levels. Moderate drinking (one to two drinks per day) can reduce testosterone levels and sperm counts, and raise the number of abnormal sperm in ejaculate. Finally, as a toxin, alcohol can kill off the sperm-generating cells in the testicle. So why take a chance? Better to cut it out.

No Caffeine or Coffee

Caffeine is another substance that needs to come off the list, in all forms: coffee, tea, chocolate (sorry) and most definitely soda. Not only does it negatively affect fertility, but it increases chances of miscarriage, increases blood pressure, and goes against the stress-free state that is so important for conception. Even decaffeinated versions of coffee and tea have some caffeine in them. Plus, with coffee, harsh chemicals are usually used in the decaffeination process, so all coffee just plain needs to be eliminated.

For those addicted, as I once was, I know how hard this step can be. If you need two to four weeks to get off caffeine, so be it. You'll sleep better, feel healthier and have more energy without it.

No Processed Sugar

Outside of alcohol, this is one of the most important ingredients to give up when trying to conceive, and for those with a sweet tooth, potentially the most difficult. Sugar negatively affects blood sugar and insulin levels, leading to hormonal imbalance. It can also compromise our immune systems. Not good at all.

Unfortunately, sugar gets added to almost everything these days, and not just the cookies and cakes. It's added to breads, cereals and a host of off-the-shelf products. If you flip over the package to read the label you might see "cane sugar," "brown sugar," "high fructose corn syrup" or just plain "sugar" listed as one of the ingredients.

Don't buy these products! Stick to whole grains, fruits and vegetables, some of which have natural sugars in them. At local health food stores, you can find wholesome products that don't contain added processed sugar—even sugar-free, wheat-free, yeast-free breads! We talk about where to find such products in the *Ingredients: What to Buy and Where to Find It* section of the *Getting Ready to Cook* chapter.

If you are having trouble eliminating sugar from your diet, try stevia. Stevia is an herb said to be 10 to 15 times sweeter than table sugar, and it has a negligible effect on blood sugar. It comes in powder or liquid form at your local health food store. Check the labels, though. In some powdered forms, maltodextrin and silica are added, and although it's a small amount, it's better to have the pure stevia extract.

Yes to Natural Sugar in Moderation

You can consume some natural sugars in moderate amounts (up to three tablespoons in a day), as they don't adversely affect blood sugar levels. These include honey, maple syrup and brown rice syrup—preferably organic and definitely all natural, meaning nothing else has been added in (check labels).

It can be difficult to tell how much of these natural sweeteners have been added to packaged foods, so I would eliminate such foods too, or consume only in small amounts, occasionally.

Whole fruits are good for you and offer a variety of nutrients. Don't consume fruit juices, though, unless you water them down and only consume in small amounts. The concentration of sugar is just too high. Jam is out for the same reason, even if it's all natural and contains only fruit and fruit juice concentrate.

No Artificial Sweeteners

Just don't do it. They're artificial and you cannot afford to put anything artificial in your body when you're trying to optimize your reproductive health.

No Dairy

This means no milk, cheese, cottage cheese or the myriad of other milk-based products out there. A number of studies link dairy to a decline in fertility.

Dairy products can have an adverse effect on endocrine and immune health. In the body, they produce galactose, a milk sugar which is apparently toxic to human eggs. Also, many adults can become sensitive to lactose, a sugar in milk, without even knowing it, and most adults lose the ability to digest lactose altogether. This means your body has to work even harder to digest dairy products, which are already hard to digest in the first place.

These are all good reasons to give up dairy. If you notice you have less mucus and generally feel better after a few weeks, you might consider giving up dairy for life.

For a milk substitution, consider almond, soy or rice milk, but check out the *Limit Soy* section in this chapter. If you find you must have dairy on occasion, go organic to avoid the hormones, among other additives.

If you worry about getting calcium, alternative sources include leafy green vegetables, such as broccoli, kale and spinach; oranges; black beans; salmon; sesame seeds and almonds.

I do make one exception in the elimination of dairy, however: yogurt, which is easier to digest than other dairy products. Organic, all natural, minimally processed yogurt with live cultures can be helpful to those suffering from candidas and yeast infections. Check labels, though, to make sure nothing is added, especially sugar!

No Wheat

The main problem with wheat is that many people have a sensitivity to it and don't even know it. This sensitivity can cause a host of problems, including inflammation, bloating, digestive issues and general fatigue, making wheat particularly hard on the body. It can also affect thyroid function, which impacts fertility.

Sensitivity aside, wheat is difficult to digest, which we don't want while trying to conceive. Wheat can also have an acidic affect on the body when we need to maintain a more alkaline pH balance for good health and fertility.

So wheat has to go. Unfortunately, eliminating wheat can mean giving up your favorite breads, baked goods, crackers, tortillas, pastas and more. Wheat can also be a "hidden" ingredient in many processed foods, such as soy sauce.

Luckily, today, there are numerous non-wheat alternatives you can find at local health food stores and on the Internet. These include non-wheat breads, rice pasta, spelt tortillas and non-wheat soy sauce. Other grains such as quinoa, rice and spelt can be substituted. Spelt is similar to wheat, but contains more protein and is easier to digest. For more information, see the section, *Ingredients: What to Buy and Where to Find It* in the *Getting Ready to Cook* chapter.

To know if a food item contains wheat, check the list of ingredients on the label. Synonyms for wheat, or other forms it can take, include: flour, white flour, whole wheat flour, semolina, durum, triticale (a hybrid of wheat and rye), bran (or wheat bran), bulgur (or bulghur wheat), graham (wheat flour), wheat germ and wheat starch. Dishes like couscous and tabbouleh are also made from wheat-based products.

The only exception I make is for wheatgrass juice, which has many health benefits, including one for fertility. See *No to Most Other Beverages* in this chapter for more information.

No to Most Processed Foods

Processed foods are those that have been altered from their natural state either for reasons of convenience or safety. As a result, most processed foods are full of preservatives, artificial ingredients, saturated fats (the "bad" fats) and/or trans fats (the really bad fats). In addition, most of the nutrients have been stripped from packaged foods through heating and other processes. All of this creates a burden for your digestive system and liver—and can tax your general health too.

What can you do? Avoid almost everything that comes in a package, can or bottle. This means no more prepared foods, especially canned meats and even sandwich meats, which typically contain nitrates or nitrites (chemical preservatives) among other additives.

Some minimally processed foods are perfectly okay, though. Rice noodles, for example, contain only rice and water, which is fine. The same goes for non-wheat pasta, such as rice pasta. An oatmeal package that contains only whole grain oats and nothing else works great. Frozen vegetables don't have the nutritional value as fresh ones, but they're better than no vegetables at all and can help if you're pressed for cooking time; just make sure the package contains only the vegetables, nothing extra.

In general, look at the list of ingredients that is on every package to make sure there are only a handful, and that all ingredients listed are those allowed on this diet. If you don't recognize an item, write it down and look it up on the Internet to learn more.

Make sure none of the packaged foods contain "partially hydrogenated vegetable oil" or "vegetable shortening" (translation: trans fats, which are particularly bad for you), preservatives, artificial flavors or colors, added sugar, or much else beyond simple, whole ingredients.

Yes to Purified Water Only

Because 70 percent of our bodies are made up of water, and water has such a healthy, alkalizing effect on our bodies, it's really important to drink at least eight 8-ounce glasses a day of clean, purified water. I emphasize "purified," because even bottled spring water can have pollutants in it, even PCP (pentachlorophenol, a contaminant from herbicides, insecticides and industrial waste sites). It's alarming, I know! During a probe into the quality of bottled water requested by the Subcommittee on Oversight and Investigations in July, 2009, subcommittee chairman, Bart Stupak (Democratic congressman, Michigan) noted that "bottled water has been recalled because of contamination by arsenic, bromate, cleaning compounds, mold and bacteria."

You just don't want these pollutants in your body when you're preparing it for a baby.

Instead, go for bottled water that has gone through a process of "reverse osmosis" or "distillation" to purify it (it should say this on the packaging), or be sure to use a good filter over your tap water. Check with the U.S. Environmental

Protection Agency (EPA) for guidelines and standards at: http://www.epa.gov/safewater/dwinfo/index.html.

A note about disposable plastic water bottles: The Food and Drug Administration (FDA) has determined that the plastic used poses no significant risk to human health because only minuscule amounts of potentially hazardous chemicals leach from the plastic into the water. However, in a 2009 study out of Germany, researchers raised doubts about this safety. The study provided evidence that estrogenic compounds (endocrine-disruptors) leach from the plastic into the water—not good for reproductive hormones. The authors of the study say additional research is needed to determine the degree of health risk this might pose to humans. Until more is known, you may want to carry water in another type of container, such as one made of glass, steal or aluminum.

No to Most Other Beverages

Most beverages on the market today contain artificial ingredients, preservatives, additives and/or added sugar. You need to stay clear from all of these, most notably sodas, even if they're sugar-free and caffeine-free. Your body does not need the artificial ingredients it contains.

Besides purified water, you can also drink herbal tea, which naturally doesn't contain caffeine. Just stay away from herbal teas that are contra-indicated for fertility or pregnancy, such as chamomile, Echinacea, St. John's wort and ginkgo biloba bayaban (the latter three for men too). Some of these herbs are not typically served as teas. Raspberry Leaf tea is said to tone the uterus and thereby aid fertility. However, there is also the belief that it induces contractions. Therefore, I would drink it while readying your body for conception and during pre-ovulation, but not post, just to be safe.

Fresh vegetable juice is wholesome and good for you. You get the most nutritional value when you make it yourself, or have it made at a juice stand, and drink it right away. The packaged variety will not have as much nutritional value, even if it's been flash pasteurized, but it won't harm. Check labels to make sure there's nothing in there except vegetables, though.

Keep in mind that juice is normally served cold and your body will need to expend extra energy to heat it for digestion. To avoid creating this extra work for your body, you can heat your juice up or at least allow it to come to room temperature, particularly on cold weather days.

On the topic of temperature, eliminate all iced and cold drinks. Ideally, you want to drink beverages closer to your body temperature. Drink water warm too.

Fruit juice needs to be avoided because of its high concentration of sugar. Eat whole fruits instead.

Finally, you may want to drink an ounce a day of wheatgrass juice. Wheatgrass juice is said to clean the blood and aid cell regeneration, and it's a good source of chlorophyll and folic acid. The high magnesium content in its chlorophyll is also said to build enzymes that restore sex hormones.

Yes to Eating Organic

Eat organic as much as possible! According to the United States Department of Agriculture (USDA), organic foods must be produced without using harmful, conventional pesticides, fertilizers that contain synthetic ingredients or sewage sludge, bioengineering, or ionizing radiation—all of which can take a toll on your body and fertility. I realize organic food is more expensive and can be harder to find, but your body needs and deserves it right now.

For produce and meat, I feel organic is a must. Much of the non-organic produce contains a large percentage of pesticides and other chemicals, and conventionally raised meat can contain growth hormones, which affect our own hormones negatively, as well as antibiotics, additives and preservatives. Also, ranchers raise conventional meat with non-organic feed that may also include other meat or beef parts. Feeding beef parts to cows has been implicated as the cause of mad cow disease. You definitely don't want any of that in your system, especially while nurturing your body for a baby.

Yes to Organic Vegetables and Fruits

If there is any category of food to go crazy on, it's vegetables. Eat as much as you like, and get a minimum of three servings a day. Vegetables provide a variety of essential vitamins and minerals, as well as fiber, and help to balance blood sugar levels, which is important to fertility. Other health benefits include lowering blood pressure; reducing risk of heart disease, stroke and cancer; and improving digestion.

Eat as much variety and as many colors as you can to get the fullest nutritional benefits. The ones that are also great sources of folic acid—which boosts fertility and helps prevent certain birth defects—include dark, leafy greens, spinach, chard, kale and celery. Nutrients included, as a group, are vitamins A, B, C, calcium, beta-carotene, iron and more.

It is best to lightly steam vegetables, which helps them release nutrients and become easier to digest. Avoid overcooking vegetables, though, as they lose nutrients that way.

Another way to eat vegetables, primarily lettuce, is in salads. Salads are served cold, so your body has to expend extra energy to digest them. Nevertheless, salads are great for cleansing the digestive system. Plus, lettuce provides a good source of vitamins and minerals. Therefore, I recommend eating salads, just not every day.

While on the subject of vegetables, I want to make a special note about potatoes. As a starch they have a "fast" effect on blood sugar, although they are also filled with nutrients. How they're prepared makes a difference. If you eat potatoes, only eat them boiled or steamed. Also keep in mind that eating them in combination with other healthy sources of fiber can mellow the effect on blood sugar.

Fruits are also full of essential vitamins as well as bioflavonoids and antioxidants, which counteract the effects of free radicals (which cause cell damage). Like vegetables, you want to eat as much variety and as many colors as possible.

Fruits, however, contain a lot of sugar, so you don't want to eat too many all at once. Limit to about four servings per day, and don't drink fruit juices, as the concentration of sugar in them is too high.

Of the many wonderful fruits, avocados are considered the fertility fruit. They're packed with folic acid and "good," heart-healthy fats, as well as great food enzymes which aid digestion.

Eat only organic vegetables and fruits. Your body can definitely do without the chemicals and pesticides found in the conventional versions.

Yes to Organic Whole Grains Other than Wheat

Whole grains contain all of their parts: the outer shell (the bran), inner portion (endosperm) and the kernel (the germ). Full of antioxidants, B vitamins and iron, they include oatmeal, brown rice, whole grain barley, wild rice, buckwheat, Kamut® and others. Whole grains can also be used as an ingredient in food, such as flour, cereal or crackers.

Whole grains provide more essential nutrients than refined grains, which are often stripped of their outer shell—although manufacturers sometimes add lost nutrients back in. Also, whole grains contain more fiber, which helps stabilize blood sugar levels—a good thing for fertility in general.

For nutritional value, try to eat as many non-wheat whole grains as possible! However, know that whole grains can be harder to digest than refined grains, such as white rice, because your digestive system has to work harder and longer to break down the grains. Also, whole grains that have been crushed into flour become easier to digest, but may subsequently lose some of their stabilizing effect on blood sugar.

What's important is the nutrition and blood sugar effect you're getting overall. If you are following the rest of this diet and eating no wheat, sugar or overly processed foods, and getting plenty of beans, vegetables and fruits, then these food choices are already helping to mellow blood sugar and provide vital nutrients. So although white rice is a refined carbohydrate, stripped of important nutrients, it's also easier for your system to digest, which we want when trying to conceive.

This is the reason all our recipes that include rice, use white basmati rice (which incidentally has a "medium" effect on blood sugar compared with regular white rice). However, feel free to mix it up occasionally by using brown rice (a whole grain), or even better, alternative grains, such as quinoa or spelt.

In summary, it's about balance! Whole grains are nutritionally better for you, no question, but a refined grain such as white rice is easier for you to digest. I just wouldn't eat mounds of it in one sitting on an empty stomach without other foods.

Yes to Organic Healthy Fats and Oils

We absolutely need fat in our bodies, particularly when trying to conceive. Fat plays an important role in our endocrine function, which regulates the hormones involved in reproduction. Fat is also the place where estrogen is manufactured and stored. So this is no time to try to lose weight on a low-fat diet! Fats can also satiate and satisfy hunger.

You should know which fats to eat, however, because there are good ones and bad ones.

The worst fat and the one to eliminate for life is trans fat. Trans fats, also listed on packaging labels as "hydrogenated oil" or "partially hydrogenated oil," are not natural and our body does not need them. Manufactured to stabilize liquid oils and prolong shelf life, these fats have found their way into an overwhelming number of packaged foods, even ones labeled "natural" or "healthy." You can also find it in margarine and in deep fried foods at restaurants. Trans fats pose serious health concerns, so check labels and cut them out.

Saturated fats, found mostly in meat and dairy products (and in small amounts in vegetable oils), increase harmful LDL cholesterol and need to be avoided. When eating meat, go for lean cuts. If you purchase processed products (which we don't recommend), such as sauces and salad dressings, check labels for saturated fat content—as well as additives and preservatives—and avoid or eliminate these. It's interesting to note that we don't need to eat saturated fat, as our bodies can produce it if we're eating enough healthy fats.

The "good" fats are the monounsaturated and polyunsaturated fats, and they have numerous health benefits when eaten in moderation, such as reducing blood pressure, stabilizing blood sugar levels, easing inflammation and, as a result, boosting fertility.

Avocados, nuts and olive oil are great sources of healthy monounsaturated fats! Omega-3 fatty acids are polyunsaturated fats that provide essential nutrients and have numerous health benefits. Your body cannot make them, so you need to get them from food. Excellent sources include flaxseeds, walnuts and seafood.

For all types of cooking, plain olive oil is best and that's what we use in all our recipes. Another good choice is canola oil, which, like olive oil, is high in monounsaturated fats and has the least saturated fat of the vegetable oils. It also has a milder flavor.

To serve cold in salads, flaxseed oil (which should never be heated), extra virgin olive oil and nut oils, such as walnut or almond, are healthy choices.

Of the olive oils, extra virgin is the healthiest, and it is safe to use for stir-frying or sautéing, but should never be used for high temperature cooking, such as deep frying or baking. At high temperatures it breaks down. We recommend using it only cold, on salads or across fresh tomatoes with basil, for example.

It is important to note that a good fat can become bad if it gets damaged by too much heat, light or oxygen. Polyunsaturated fats tend to be the most fragile, so oils that are high in polyunsaturated fats, such as flaxseed, safflower and sunflower, should be refrigerated. Their packaging should indicate this. All oils should be stored in a dark, cool place. Organic oils are best.

Yes to Organic, Lean Meat and Poultry

Meat and poultry provide a high level of protein, selenium and certain B vitamins, which are important to fertility for both men and women. Rich in iron, beef is also good for the blood. If you eat meat, though, it *has* to be organic. The organic variety is free of antibiotics and growth hormones, which can affect our own hormones and, in turn, adversely affect fertility. You definitely don't want that!

In order to label meat organic, ranchers must also provide livestock with organic, vegetarian feed that is free of chemicals, additives and genetically modified foods. The result makes life easier on our digestive and immune systems.

You also need to eat only lean meat. Either buy it that way or be sure to trim off any fat. The main reason is that long-term pesticide residues—which cannot be eradicated by organic farming methods—almost all settle in the fat of the animal. Nasty dioxins, the toxic byproducts of manufacturing that are eventually consumed by animals, also concentrate in the fat. Dioxins can impact the immune system and have been linked to fertility issues for both men and women. So, eat meat lean!

In the case of poultry, don't eat the skin either, which can also retain chemicals.

If you are having an especially difficult time locating organic meat, I offer this: if it's all natural, meaning that it doesn't contain antibiotics, growth hormones, preservatives or additives, and if the animals have been eating an all-vegetable feed, that's what's most important. If the feed itself is not organic, that's not as important.

If you're buying from the butcher, ask about antibiotics and growth hormones. Ask whether it's organic. Whole Foods Market sells organic chicken and beef. For the all natural variety, a company called Niman Ranch appears to do a great job and sells online, but there are others. Search the Internet.

If you're buying packaged raw meat, check the label. "Organic" implies specific guidelines and rules, but "Natural" does not, as that term gets loosely interpreted. If you're not sure what's in the meat, call the number on the package and ask. Remember: This is your body we're talking about—and this is a baby you're making!

In the case of red meat, limit to one or two servings per week, as it is higher in saturated fat and is harder to digest. For poultry, choose light meat, such as the breast, which is lower in fat and easier to digest than dark meat. For pork, go for only fresh lean cuts, such as tenderloin, loin chops and sirloin roast. Skip the bacon and all other fatty or processed versions of pork.

A quick word about processed meat: No! Absolutely do not consume them! I'm talking about hot dogs, canned chicken and most sandwich meat. They're processed and contain preservatives, additives, nitrates or nitrites (in most sandwich meats), and sometimes other inferior meat products, such as spinal cord or bits of brain. You don't want any of that in your body right now.

Also, don't eat raw or undercooked meat, which can harbor bacteria.

Yes to Seafood, But Limit

Because of mercury levels, you need to limit seafood to once or twice per week, which is a shame because fish is an excellent source of omega-3 fatty acids, an important and healthy fat, B vitamins and lean protein. Seafood is also abundant in essential minerals, including iron, zinc, iodine and selenium. Oysters are also a good source of zinc, an important mineral to both male and female fertility.

When choosing seafood, stick to those which contain the lowest levels of mercury, such as Pacific halibut and wild Pacific salmon. For a list of which seafood is safest, check the easy-to-read Seafood Watch® guide on the Monterey Bay Aquarium web site at: http://www.montereybayaquarium.org/cr/SeafoodWatch/web/sfw_regional.aspx.

Also, don't eat raw fish, including sushi, which can harbor bacteria.

Yes to Nuts and Seeds

Nuts and seeds are fantastic fertility foods. They provide a great source of protein and healthy fats, which help stabilize blood sugar levels, ease inflammation and boost fertility. Nuts and seeds also contain essential minerals and fiber, which is important for the health of the digestive system and lowering cholesterol.

For seeds, good choices are pumpkin and sesame, both of which are high in healthy monounsaturated fats and good sources of zinc, which is important for male and female reproduction.

Flaxseeds provide an abundant amount of omega-3 fats, which your body needs and can't produce on its own. They come whole, ground or in the form of flaxseed oil, which is great served cold as a salad dressing (never heat flaxseed oil!). In addition, flaxseeds are a good source of folate.

For nuts, the best choices are almonds and walnuts. Almonds are a great source of healthy monounsaturated fats while walnuts are an excellent source of important omega-3 fats—along with essential nutrients. Peanuts are also a good source of healthy fats, minerals and a significant amount of folate. However, peanuts can be allergenic to some people.

Nuts and seeds can be sprinkled on salads or added to oatmeal. Eaten raw and whole, nuts in particular do create more work for your body's digestion; however, their numerous health benefits, especially for fertility, make them well worth eating. You can soak almonds in water to make them easier to digest. Crushing nuts before adding to foods also makes them easier to digest.

Buy and eat organic, raw nuts and seeds and store in the refrigerator for freshness. Because they're high in fat, albeit healthy fat, you don't want to eat too many; two ounces (about a ½ cup in volume) a day at most.

Yes to Beans and Other Legumes, Except Peas

Beans and legumes are one of the most fertility friendly foods available. Not only are they packed with protein, fiber and important nutrients such as calcium, iron and potassium, but they also contain a high percentage of folate, which boosts fertility in both men and women and helps prevent certain birth defects. Low in fat, beans are also great for digestion and the heart, and their high fiber content helps stabilize blood sugar levels.

Beans are also a great source of antioxidants. The darker the bean's seed coat, the higher its level of antioxidant activity, with black beans having the most, followed by red, brown, yellow and white beans.

Definitely eat your beans, but not your peas. Peas contain a natural contraceptive (m-xylohydroquinine) which interferes with estrogen and progesterone. So pass on the peas, including snow peas.

Limit Soy

Because soybeans are the only vegetable to contain a complete set of amino acids, they make a great source of protein, equivalent to meat and eggs. They're also a good source of magnesium, iron, omega-3 fatty acids and more, and have been tooted for a number of health benefits.

When you give up dairy, you might be tempted to load up instead on soy milk, soy cheese, tofu, tempeh, soy burgers, soy chips and so on. Be careful, though. Not only are a lot of these processed foods, but soybeans contain isoflavones, which mimic estrogen. Consumed in large or concentrated amounts, this can have a serious negative impact on fertility. Also, processed soy (the soy burgers, soy chips and so on) has been connected to impaired mineral absorption and thyroid dysfunction, both of which you don't need while trying to conceive.

If you eat soy, do so only occasionally, no more than three servings per week. Stick with whole soy foods, like tofu, soy milk and edamame, over other forms for greater nutritional value. Finally, avoid processed soy and opt instead for the fermented variety. Research demonstrates that traditional preparation methods, including the use of traditionally fermented soy products such as tofu, miso and soy sauce, are best when it comes to our health.

Drink Water Separately

The hydrochloric acid in your stomach works to break down your food. If you're chugging large amounts of water, or another beverage, during your meal, it interferes with digestion. Instead, drink water a full hour before your meal so that it doesn't interfere with digestion, and wait at least an hour afterwards to drink again. Small sips during your meal are okay, though.

Balance Your pH

Our bodies work best, and are healthiest, in a slightly alkaline environment. Unfortunately, dairy (which is not allowed), meat and nuts, along with stressful living habits, can have an acidic effect on the body's pH balance, which isn't good for fertility. Microorganisms such as yeast, bacteria, viruses and others thrive in an acidic environment, and these can indirectly affect the balance of hormones critical to reproduction in both men and women. To tilt your body to an alkalizing environment:

- Drink a warm glass of purified water with lemon squeezed into it first thing every morning. Give it 15 or 20 minutes before eating or drinking something else.

- Drink at least eight 8-ounce glasses of purified water a day.

- Eat plenty of vegetables, which are good alkalizers.

Boost Male Fertility

In addition to following the dietary guidelines recommended here for a nutritionally balanced diet, if you are the male partner, you want to be sure that you get sufficient levels of zinc, selenium, vitamin B12 and vitamin C. These nutrients help you produce healthy, viable sperm. Good sources of these include the following:

- Selenium – Brazil nuts, snapper, cod, halibut, salmon, shrimp, barley, lean lamb.

- Vitamin B12 – lean beef, lean lamb, shrimp, salmon, snapper, scallops.

- Zinc – lean beef, pork and lamb, sesame seeds, pumpkin seeds and shrimp.

- Vitamin C – bell peppers, broccoli, Brussels sprouts, strawberries, oranges and more. Instead of orange juice, which provides too much concentrated sugar, eat whole oranges or grapefruits.

Lifestyle Factors

As mentioned previously, diet does not work alone. It's also important to get plenty of rest, reduce stress and avoid toxins. It also helps to get mind, body and spirit in a calm, nurturing place. Here are a few suggestions.

Reduce Stress

Reducing stress can be challenging while coping with fertility issues, which itself is highly stressful, but it is vital. Stress is fertility's worst enemy. You need to eliminate it, and if that fails, you need to train yourself to respond to stress in a healthy manner.

Some of the methods I used and suggest to you are the following. If you find you don't have the patience for them, consider that you *really* need them, as was the case with me. Like anything new, give yourself time to adjust. When I started, I couldn't meditate for five seconds, let alone 20 minutes. I just kept at it.

- Deep breathing, in through the nose, out through the mouth slowly, 10 times. While you do this, you can count, or repeat the mantra, "I am at peace." This is helpful when you're about to see your fertility specialist and find your heart racing. Stop and take a moment to breathe deeply.

- Meditation. Aim for 20 minutes a day. Sit straight in a comfortable, quiet place, breathe slowly and consciously and attempt to empty your mind.

- Yoga. Although I admire yoga, I'm not into it, and only did it to aid fertility. That being said, my favorite routine, which I practiced three times per week, is Brenda Strong's *Yoga 4 Fertility* DVD. It's gentle and geared specifically for fertility.

During this challenging time, it's important to find time to put your health and well-being first.

Avoid Toxins, Especially Cigarette Smoke

If you smoke there is nothing better you can do than to quit. Eating right and reducing your stress are cancelled out by the numerous ill effects of smoking. Seek whatever help you need, but make this a priority.

Aside from smoking, avoid any known toxins in your work and home environment, such as pesticides and cleaning products.

Maintain a Healthy Body Mass Index

We know that being grossly overweight or underweight negatively impacts fertility, but is there a healthy weight range that is optimal? Yes! Researchers have determined that a Body Mass Index of between 20 and 24 is ideal for fertility.

Body Mass Index (BMI) is calculated by dividing your weight in pounds by the square of your height in inches and then multiplying by 703. So if you are 125 pounds and are 5 feet, 5 inches (or 65 inches), your BMI = (125 divided by (65 x 65)) x 703 = 21. To help, use the BMI calculator found at http://www.nhlbisupport.com/bmi/. A metric version is available here: http://www.nhlbisupport.com/bmi/bmi-m.htm.

If your BMI is under 20 or over 24, do not binge or crash diet to get to your desired weight. This is stressful for the body. Instead, work on losing or gaining weight slowly over the course of many weeks, and consult your doctor for more information.

Exercise Moderately

Moderate exercise is great for oxygenating the blood and circulating it through the whole body, including the reproductive area. I recommend three to six days a week of exercise, such as walking, biking or swimming, for at least 30 minutes. Intense or rigorous exercise, however, is not a good idea. My fertility clinic recommended I keep my heart rate at or below 120 beats per minute during treatment. Exercise, but keep it mellow and gentle.

Use the Power of Visualizations and Affirmations

Coping with fertility issues can be extremely challenging and draining. Throughout the process, it's important to get plenty of rest and nurture yourself. Many find the following tools useful.

- Visualization is a powerful healing method. You can visualize the end result you desire repeatedly, or visualize healing, such as a bright, golden light filling your uterus. Search the Internet for fertility-related CD's. My favorite is Julia Indichova's Fertile Heart™ Imagery, found on her web site at www. fertileheart.com.

- Affirmations help keep our thoughts focused on positive results.

When following the guidelines, I encourage you to give yourself time to adapt to the changes, enjoy the healthy eating, and celebrate how you feel as a result. Keep in mind that if there's any time in life to nurture yourself, it's now, and you deserve it.

QUICK GUIDE TO FERTILE KITCHEN™ DIETARY GUIDELINES

YES	NO	LIMIT
Eating Organic	Alcohol	Seafood, low mercury options only, 1 or 2 times per week
Vegetables and Fruits	Caffeine	
Meat and Poultry	Coffee, even decaffeinated	Red Meat, 1 or 2 times per week
Whole Grains other than wheat, such as rye, Kamut® and spelt	Processed Sugar	Natural Sugars, such as honey, maple syrup and brown rice syrup (up to 3 Tbsp in a day)
White Rice, easier to digest	Artificial Sweeteners	
Beans	Dairy	Yogurt, organic, all natural with live cultures, helpful to those who have candidas or yeast infections
Nuts and Seeds, especially walnuts, almonds and flaxseeds	Wheat	
Vegetable Oils, such as olive and canola oil	Most Processed Foods	Soy, 3 times per week at most, choose fermented soy over processed soy
Purified Water, warm	Trans Fat	
Vegetable Juice, warm	Sodas and Other Bottled Beverages	Raspberry Leaf Tea, only in pre-ovulation
Wheatgrass Juice	Fruit Juice, too much sugar	Potatoes, boiled or steamed only
Herbal tea, except those contra-indicated for fertility or pregnancy	Iced or Cold Beverages	Herbs, always check if contra-indicated for fertility or pregnancy before using
	Chamomile Tea	
Minimally processed foods, such as rice noodles or frozen vegetables	Peas, a natural contraceptive	
	Raw Meat or Fish	

Getting Ready to Cook

Pierre writes:

Before starting in on the recipes, you may want to peruse this chapter for basic cooking tips, guidelines and reference information. In the following sections, this is what you'll find:

- Cooking Basics – Tips to make the process go easier; information on what equipment to use, including the most suitable type of pans; standard cooking terms; and relevant conversion tables for easy reference.

- Ingredients: What to Buy and Where to Find It – We highlight products that may be hard to find, such as wheat-free products, and make suggestions on where to find them.

- Substitutions and Creativity – Tips on making substitutions in recipes and using creativity to go off of them.

- Spices – A list of common spices you can use to accent and create your own dishes.

Cooking Basics

This section includes basic information to know before, during and after cooking.

Preparing to Cook

Before you begin to work on any recipe, and while working on it, we recommend you do the following. This will make the cooking easier and go more smoothly.

- Clear your kitchen workspace, countertops and stove, if they are not clear already.

- Read the recipe all the way through, making sure you understand every step and that all equipment, utensils and ingredients needed are available.

- Set aside in one place all needed ingredients and utensils, so you don't have to look for something while cooking, which can be stressful.

- Prepare all ingredients in advance by chopping, cutting, dicing, opening cans and packages and so on, so that everything will be ready when you need it.

- Clean up as you go. Put waste in the trash, wash pots and pans, clean countertops, rinse dishes and bowls and put items away when you don't need them anymore. However, keep in mind that the priority is cooking; clean up as cooking allows.

Useful Cooking Tips
The following tips are useful when cooking in general or around the kitchen.

- Use scissors to cut fresh herbs.

- You can often double or halve portions of a recipe just by doubling or halving the ingredients used in it.

- To open a jar with a tight lid, run hot water over the lid for a few seconds. Thermal expansion of the metal lid will make it less tight.

- For convenience, freeze any leftovers in plastic or zip-lock bags, by portions. For example, you can cook six portions of a meal and freeze four of them in two separate bags for two future occasions.

    You can also do the same for raw food. For example, you can freeze two chicken breasts, already cut and ready to cook, in its plastic bag, separate from a larger package, for convenience. Make sure plastic bags are well-sealed before placing in the freezer.

- Rub a lemon slice on your hands to remove stains and strong odors.

- In case of burn, put your hand under running cold water for several minutes or hold an ice cube on the burned area.

- To re-heat prepared food (that is not soup or primarily liquid), do the following: Bring a small amount of water (2 Tbsp) in a pot to boil on high heat. Place the prepared food in this boiling water, cover, and wait until steam fills the pot and the water starts to boil again. Remove from heat and let sit, covered, for about two minutes, depending on how much food you put in with the water. Serve. If the food item is liquid, such as a soup, just warm on medium heat. When it starts to boil, it's ready to serve.

NOTE: Avoid using the microwave to reheat food, as it can remove some of the nutrients.

Equipment to Use

You should have the following basic items available for cooking and clean up.

- **Pots and pans.** For most cooking, the following basics work great. I end up using the same pots and pans in all my cooking. Invest in good quality ones and they will keep for many years.

  - **Saucepan**, standard size, non-stick – This type of pan has straight or flared sides and can be deep or shallow. It's versatile and can be used for soups, sauces, sautéing and more. It comes with a tight-fitting lid.

  - **Skillet** (or frying pan), standard size, non-stick – This pan has low, gently sloping sides and is used to fry, sauté, stir fry, make eggs and other uses.

  - **Pots**, one large and one medium – This is a round, deep cooking container that has a lid. It's used for higher volume stews and soups, and can come in small, medium and large sizes.

  - **Steamer**, either as a basket that you can place inside a pot with a lid or a full steamer. Usually used to steam vegetables.

NOTE: Non-stick skillets and saucepans are much easier to work with and enable cooks to use much less oil (for frying or sautéing) than they would otherwise. Ones made of cast iron or other materials are also good. However, keep in mind that they can require more maintenance, foods tend to stick to their surfaces and burn more easily, and you will need to add more oil, water or broth to them for cooking.

NOTE: Also keep in mind that non-stick pans can have a limited life because once they get scratched, they need to be replaced for safety reasons. (Trace amounts of a hazardous chemical may be released with scratches.)

To avoid scratches, never use metal of any kind in these pans, including silverware and especially steal wool, which should never be used to clean non-stick pans. Use only plastic or wooden spoons and spatulas to mix and stir food in them. Also, don't stack non-stick cookware on top of each other, and always wash by hand. Although today's non-stick coated pans are tougher than ever and can withstand less careful handling than previous generations, it's better to be safe.

Also, never leave a non-stick pan on full high heat with nothing in it. This will cause the coating to release toxic fumes and ruin the pan, which will then need to be replaced.

- **Cutting board.** Wood is preferred, as it is a natural material. Always clean both sides of the board, getting both sides wet, and never let it sit flat in water. Wood that expands from water on one side only will bend and/or break.

- **Cutting knife.** A good knife with a blade of about 20 inches long allows you to cut most items without having to do a partial cut. Standard knives have blades which are too short for cooking purposes. Sharpen your knife before each meal preparation using sharpening steel or similar tool. (There is nothing worse than trying to cut or mince ingredients with a dull knife.) Always rinse the knife after sharpening to remove small metal residue.

- **Chopping device** (optional), such as a food processor or simple mechanical tool that cuts onions or apples, for example. This is not required, but useful, particularly when preparing ingredients for a salad (for cutting or shredding carrots, cabbage and onions), or preparing large quantities of food.

- **Measuring cups and spoons.** Unless you cook by taste and are used to using spices (and other items) in particular amounts, these tools are absolutely necessary to follow a recipe.

- **Scale.** A small plastic scale (handling a minimum of up to 1 lb) is sufficient, and is useful for weighing ingredients listed in ounces, which is a weight measurement. Although we try to provide the equivalent in cups for most ingredients, or the weight can be read on packages, a scale is still very useful for weighing some of the ingredients in our recipes. Without a scale, you will need to refer to the conversion table for approximate equivalents.

- **Timer.** You will need to set a timer and hear it ring for key steps in the cooking process. Looking at your watch is not enough. You will want to hear a reminder, for example, of when pasta has finished cooking and needs to be immediately removed from the heat.

- **Spatulas**, wooden and plastic. I prefer wooden spatulas, which are stiffer, to stir and mix items. However, to flip items such as eggs, a thin plastic spatula is necessary. Avoid using metal spatulas in non-stick pans, as they can cause unwanted scratches to the non-stick surface.

- **Kitchen towels and sponge.** Have these items ready. You will need them to dry utensils you just rinsed (towel 1), dry your hands after washing them (towel 2), and clean up counter tops and utensils (sponge).

- **Bowls, plates, silverware and serving dish.** Food always tastes better when it is well-presented. A very small effort can make a big difference.

- **Tupperware, aluminum foil, plastic sandwich bags and jars.** Use these items to store leftovers. Avoid putting hot foods in plastic containers, though. Let them cool off first. You can cool foods off quickly by running them under cold water or placing them on a plate in the refrigerator. Store leftovers in the refrigerator for up to three days, or in the freezer. However, don't use aluminum foil or glass for items to be stored in the freezer and ensure seals are tight.

Common Cooking Terms
We include a handful of the more common cooking terms.

- **Boil** – To cook in water or another liquid on high heat while the liquid is bubbling vigorously.

- **Simmer** – To keep the temperature of a liquid just below boiling so that only small bubbles gently rise to the surface. To simmer, first bring liquid to a boil, and then lower and adjust temperature until you see small bubbles, gently rising. You can also simmer by raising the temperature slowly.

- **Steam** – To cook in steam by suspending the food (usually vegetables) *over* but not *in* boiling water using a basket within a pot or a steamer. Cover tightly to keep the steam inside. If you don't have a basket or steamer, you can still steam food by placing it in a *very small amount* of boiling water in a pan and covering. Remove from heat before the water boils completely away.

- **Poach** – To cook the food completely submerged in barely simmering water or liquid. Example: poached eggs.

- **Sauté** – To cook in a small amount of healthy oil on high heat in a pan or skillet, stirring frequently to prevent burning. Usually this is a short process that keeps the food items colorful and juicy. NOTE: For a light sauté, use vegetable broth instead of oil. Be sure to add more broth as needed to ensure there is always some liquid in the pan.

- **Marinate** – To submerge meat, seafood and/or vegetables in a liquid made up of spices and other seasonings, and let sit for a certain amount of time in order for the food to absorb the flavors and become more tender.

- **Roast** – A method of cooking in an oven with the food item uncovered so that dry heat can surround the item. When roasting large pieces of meat, such as a turkey, use a meat thermometer to check for readiness (180 degrees for poultry, 170 degrees for well-done beef, 160 degrees for medium beef or lamb).

- **Chop** – To cut into irregular pieces of no set size. A particular chopping technique involves quick movements of a sharp knife, but you should not try this unless you are experienced with a knife.

- **Dice** – To cut into small cubes. (They don't have to be exactly uniform.)

- **Mince** – To cut into very small, or fine, pieces.

Food Quantities Table

The following table provides the amounts in ounces as well as grams (or deciliters) that constitute one serving of sample foods listed.

	oz	dl or g	
Soup side	7 to 9	2 to 2.5	dl
Soup main	11 to 14	3 to 4	dl
Sauce	2 to 3	0.6 to 0.9	dl
Meat	6 to 7	170 to 200	g
Fish	7	200	g
Salad	3.5	100	g
Vegetable	7	200	g
Pasta side	3	80	g
Pasta main	6	150	g
Rice, Corn	3	80	g
Fruits	6	150	g
Drinks	10	3	dl

Conversion Tables

volume					
oz	cup	TBSP	tsp	ml / cc	dl
½	¹⁄₁₆	1	3	14.2	0.142
2	¼	4			0.57
4	½	5			1.14
8	1	16	48	227	2.27
16	2				4.54
24	3				6.81
32	4				9.08

temperature	
°F	°C
32	0
77	25
100	37.8
212	100
300	149
350	177
400	204
450	232
500	260

weight		
oz	lbs	g
1	¹⁄₁₆	28.35
4	¼	113
8	½	227
16	1	454
35.28	2.205	1000

3	teaspoons	=	1	tablespoon		
4	tablespoons	=	¼	cup		
12	tablespoons	=	¾	cup		
16	tablespoons	=	1	cup		
1	cup	=	8	ounces		
2	cups	=	1	pint	=	16 ounces
4	cups	=	1	quart	=	32 ounces
4	quarts	=	1	gallon	=	128 ounces

Ingredients: What to Buy and Where to Find It

If you have never gone without processed sugar, wheat or dairy before, or eaten only organic meats, knowing what to eat and where to find it may be a challenge. This section provides some guidance.

First, a few general tips about the ingredients in our recipes and shopping for them.

- Use organic, fresh ingredients as much as possible, or organic frozen if you can't get fresh, or if it's more convenient. Do not use canned food items, except for organic canned tomatoes or beans, for convenience.

- To freeze fresh vegetables, preserving them for extended use, boil or steam them for two minutes, and then freeze.

- Because most pre-packaged, prepared foods are not allowed, make your own tomato sauces, soups and salad dressings, unless you can find packaged organic versions of these that have no preservatives, additives, wheat, dairy or added sugar. Refer to our recipes for some of these items.

- *Always check labels.* The label of a package or can always lists ingredients in order of its highest content first. Make sure the package contains mostly organic ingredients with no preservatives, additives, wheat, dairy or added sugar. (As a carbohydrate, rice, for example, contains natural sugar, but no additional sugar should be added to any package of rice.) If you don't understand an item in the list, write it down and search for it on the Internet to learn more. Otherwise, don't buy it.

- Locate a good, local health food store, and do most of your shopping there. You will learn where to find certain items on shelves, and thereby save time shopping. Ask shop clerks for help and don't waste time looking for specific items they may not carry. For additional places to shop, see information in the rest of this section.

NOTE: Today, many organic foods can also be found at regular grocery stores, so check there too. You can also look in your area for local retailers of natural and organic foods. Finally, you can always search the Internet for a reliable online health food store or shop for particular products by manufacturer.

Locating Organic Fruits and Vegetables

Check local farmer's markets and look for organic labels or ask if produce is organic. In certain parts of the country, the produce section in your regular grocery will offer organic choices. Also, look for organic produce at your local health food store. In many cities and towns, there are companies that offer service delivery of organic produce from local farms, such as Planet Organics at www.planetorganics.com or Boxed Greens at www.boxedgreens.com. There are many others.

Locating More Exotic Items

For items such as rice flour, wheat-free soy sauce, rice noodles or tahini paste (ground sesame seeds), check the Asian or Middle-Eastern sections of your grocery stores. If those don't exist, check in your local health food store, at a specialty Asian or Middle-Eastern market, or shop online.

NOTE: Non-wheat soy sauce may be difficult to find. In our local health food store, we found one manufactured by San-J called "Organic Tamari Wheat-Free Soy Sauce."

Locating Non-Wheat Products and Alternative Grains

Wheat seems to be in everything, such as breads, pastas, cereals, crackers and snack foods. What do we do? Luckily, today you can find non-wheat alternatives for all these items made from other grains, such as rice, Kamut®, quinoa, rye, spelt, oats and others, available at most local health food stores.

For breads, check labels carefully to ensure there is no wheat or added sugar, because manufacturers will sometimes mix wheat flour in with the whole grain. In other words, make sure your rye bread is made of 100 percent rye. Breads that are also yeast-free will often be found in the refrigerator section of your health food or grocery store.

You can also find pasta made with brown rice, quinoa, spelt or Kamut®.

Here are just a handful of products we use and have found at our local health food store in California. We also list some manufacturers to help you locate these products in your area. IMPORTANT: We are not in any way endorsing these products or manufacturers, and they represent a fraction of the many available in the marketplace today.

- Crackers – Mary's Gone Crackers® and Brown Rice Snaps™
- Lundberg Family Farms (http://www.lundberg.com/) for organic rice cakes

- Breads (sugar-free, wheat-free, yeast-free) – Organic 100% Rye Bread with Flax Seed made by French Meadow Bakery (www.frenchmeadow.com)

- Arrowhead Mills (http://www.arrowheadmills.com/), which provides non-wheat, organic pancake mixes, organic green lentils, organic chickpeas and more

- Eden Organic (http://www.edenfoods.com/)

- Bob's Red Mill (http://www.bobsredmill.com/) for oatmeal and other products

Also check on our website at www.fertilekitchen.com for more information and updates.

Substitutions and Creativity

There are different reasons you may want to substitute ingredients in recipes. One is that you may not have on hand a particular item and would like to substitute it for an equivalent, such as rice milk for soy milk, or corn flour for rice flour. Another reason is that you want to experiment and create something new, by using strawberries for blueberries, for example, or replacing one type of spice with another. Of course, you may also wish to substitute a food not supported in our guidelines, such as dairy or wheat, for your own nutritional needs or dietary beliefs, which is perfectly fine.

In following our recipes, here are some equivalent substitutions you can make for common ingredients and still support our dietary guidelines:

- For rice flour you can substitute corn flour, although we prefer you stick with rice flour. You can also experiment with other non-wheat flours. (However, make sure that wheat has not been mixed in.)

- For soy milk you can substitute rice milk or almond milk. Use organic, unsweetened varieties.

- For olive oil you can substitute canola oil, for cooking.

- For dry mushrooms you can substitute fresh ones.

- For fresh spices you can substitute dry ones, and vice versa. One (1) Tbsp of dry spice is roughly equal to about 3 Tbsp of fresh.

- Although fresh is preferred, for convenience or availability, you can substitute frozen vegetables for fresh ones.

- For canned tomatoes, you can substitute fresh ones, and vice versa. One 10 oz can of tomatoes is roughly equal to about two fresh tomatoes, depending on the size and type of tomatoes. You can also weigh the fresh tomatoes and use about 12 oz of them as an equivalent to the 10 oz can.

Feel free to use your imagination and get creative with these recipes. Here's how: Follow a recipe two or three times, and then try it without reading the recipe. This will allow for small variations. Next, try to vary the spices, or substitute one for another. You can also try changing the type of meat or vegetables used, or adding something that was not in the original recipe. Taking this approach will give you a feel for what to do or not do—and you will be on your way to creating your own recipes.

Let us know how it goes. Visit www.fertilekitchen.com to post your own recipes, or comment on the recipe you just did.

Spices

Spices have been used for centuries to flavor dishes and are considered the key to cooking. Historically, they were rare and hard to find. Today, you can find almost any spice year round. Be careful not to overuse spices, however, or use too many of them together; otherwise, they may overpower the original flavors of the meat and vegetables. Instead, use them to enrich and accent flavors.

Use fresh, organic spices whenever possible, and don't keep dry spices for more than a year.

- **Salt.** Use rock salt. Avoid sea salt, as it doesn't contain iodine, and with a diet free of dairy and processed food, you may need supplemental iodine.

- **Pepper.** We use black pepper in our recipes, but there is also green and white pepper. To ensure no additives, buy whole pepper corns and grind them in a pepper grinder as you prepare food. You can measure how many grinder turns correspond to ¼ teaspoon so that you won't have to measure the pepper for recipes and just count grinder turns instead.

- **Paprika.** This is a colorful, mild spice that's perfect for poultry. It comes dry in powder form.

- **Basil.** Use fresh basil as much as possible. You can freeze the leaves, or maintain freshness by keeping the stems in a glass of water, as you would for flowers. It's good for vegetables, pasta, tomatoes and almost every dish.

- **Cilantro.** This fresh and tasty herb can be used raw or very lightly cooked. Freeze the leaves or keep the stems in a glass of water.

- **Dill.** This spice, found fresh or dry at the store, is a great choice for fish.

- **Turmeric.** This powdered spice is known for its anti-inflammatory properties and used for many medicinal purposes, including painful menstruation, in Indian and Chinese culture. It's colorful and not as spicy hot as some of the other spices used in curry powder.

- **Curry.** Curry is a mix of many spices and comes as either a powder or a paste. Their spiciness ranges from mild to very hot. If very hot, you can mix with turmeric to cut the spiciness. If you buy this spice in an Indian store, it is likely to be spicier (hotter).

- **Sage.** This is a great spice for stews. You can also drink it as tea. As leaves, they are available fresh or dry.

- **Bay leaves.** These are great for stews and long cooking vegetable mixes.

- **Parsley.** Parsley is great with vegetables and in soups. Freeze or keep the stems in a glass of water. Buy fresh, although it's also available dry.

- **Cayenne pepper.** This dry, powder spice supports the immune system, acts as a natural pain reliever and provides beta carotene and vitamin A. Use carefully, as it is very hot, so you don't need to add much to foods.

- **Oregano.** A great spice for soups and tomato dishes. Buy it dry at the store.

- **Cloves.** Great for stews. Buy it dry at the grocery store.

- **Thyme.** This spice is said to fight bacteria and be good for respiratory problems. It also functions as an antioxidant with many other benefits. You can find it fresh or dry at the grocery store.

- **Saffron.** This dry, powder spice is good for rice and fish.

- **Rosemary.** This spice is available fresh or dry, and is great for various meat dishes.

- **Mustard.** You may think of mustard more as a condiment than a spice, but the crushed mustard seeds that make up mustard pastes are great for sauces, or as a side for roasted meats. Use only high-end mustard, such as Dijon mustard, which contains only vinegar and mustard.

- **Ginger.** You can find this root plant in the produce section of most grocery stores. Used in a lot of Asian-inspired cooking, it has a strong taste and comes with many health benefits.

- **Mixed herbs.** A couple of common mixed herbs which we use in our recipes are **Italian herbs** and **Herbs de Provence**. These mixed herbs consist of a combination of herbs and spices, with each packaged brand offering a little different variation on the same combination of herbs and spices than another.

  - **Italian herbs** usually consists of marjoram, thyme, rosemary, savory, sage, oregano and basil, and could also have garlic, onion, dill and tarragon.

  - **Herbs de Provence** usually consists of basil, rosemary, marjoram, savory and thyme, but can also include lavender and fennel.

With that brief run-down of common spices, we are ready to cook

The Fertile Kitchen™ Recipes

Pierre writes:

As mentioned earlier, these healthy, easy-to-make recipes evolved from my own creative enthusiasm to support both my wife and myself in our efforts to conceive.

The result is this collection of flavorful, ethnically diverse dishes. They include favorites such as *Lamb Curry in Coconut Milk, Crêpes Salée, Spicy Garbanzo Beans* and a light version of *Chili Con Carne*. Few would guess these dishes contain no sugar or wheat, or other restrictive qualities—and that would be the point!

All recipes use a similar, consistent format and include full color photos so they are simple to read and follow. Keep the following important points in mind when following these recipes:

- All produce, meat, oil and grain products, such as rice and pasta, are assumed to be ORGANIC, even though we don't explicitly write this in the recipes. Organic is especially important for meat and produce. For other ingredients, try to use organic as much as possible.

- In addition, meat used in recipes is assumed to be boneless and skinless. If you didn't buy it lean, you will need to trim the fat.

- For simplicity, we use the same choice of quality products throughout, such as olive oil and rice flour (although other oils and flours can be used).

- To keep the preparation and cooking processes as simple as possible, we offer some shortcuts, such as using organic packaged oatmeal or a pancake mix, and canned tomatoes instead of fresh.

- Although fresh is better, you can use frozen if that's more convenient or if that's what's available.

Now, let's start cooking!

Breakfast

Breakfast is the most important meal of the day. Without it you run low on fuel, which is stressful for the body. So don't skip it! Just eat the right foods. Instead of processed sugar and refined carbohydrates, include sources of protein and fiber.

In this section, we include a fresh, flavor-rich spinach and mushroom omelet to which you can substitute your own choice of vegetables. Whole grain breads and cereals also make great breakfast choices. You can enliven a bowl of oatmeal with raisins, berries or crushed nuts, and sweeten it with honey. Pancakes made from 100 percent whole grain, such as Kamut® can put the fun back in breakfast. Throw in fresh blueberries and dribble honey or all natural maple syrup on top to sweeten.

Spinach and Mushroom Omelet

This is a great, classic omelet dish. You can easily replace its fillings with other vegetables.

1
The finished dish

2
Ingredients

Ingredients:

3 eggs

2 Tbsp soy milk

¼ tsp salt and pepper

4 mushrooms, sliced

10 leaves of baby spinach

1 tsp olive oil

EASY

Preparation time: 5 min.
Cooking time: 5 min.
Serves 1 to 2

Recipe:

1. Place eggs and soy milk in a medium-size mixing bowl and beat together.

2. Add salt and pepper.

3. Place olive oil in a non-stick skillet on medium heat.

4. Add egg mixture (pict. 3) and tip the pan to spread the egg mixture throughout the bottom of the pan.

5. Cook for 3 minutes, until eggs appear mostly cooked, but with some liquid egg on top (pict. 4).

6. Tip pan again to bring the liquid to the edges, and then add spinach and sliced mushrooms to half the omelet (pict. 5).

   SUGGESTION: For an alternative filling, you can also use onions, tomatoes and/or chives. You can also pre-cook the filling (onions, spinach, or tomatoes), or use them raw (spinach, mushrooms, tomatoes and chives).

7. Use a spatula to close the omelet in half (pict. 6).

8. Let cook for a couple of minutes more.

9. Serve.

Adding egg mixture

Ready to fill and turn

Adding the filling

Closing the omelet

Blueberry Pancakes

Who doesn't like blueberry pancakes? These are made with a wholesome grain called Kamut®, which gives them a lighter taste and feel. For convenience and ease, we used a pancake mix with all healthy ingredients from Arrowhead Mills®. Look for it at your local health food store or order it online. The recipe is a small variation from the one on the package.

The finished dish

Ingredients:

1 cup of Arrowhead Mills® Kamut® Pancake & Waffle Mix

2 Tbsp honey

2 Tbsp olive oil

1 cup + 2 Tbsp soy milk

1 cup fresh blueberries

2 more Tbsp olive oil to oil pan

EASY ⊗ ⊗ ⊗

Preparation time: 5 min.
Cooking time: 20 to 30 min.
Serves 4 to 6

Recipe:

1. In a medium or large mixing bowl, add pancake mix, honey, soy milk and 2 Tbsp of olive oil.

2. Stir well until the lumps disappear.

3. Add blueberries and stir into the pancake mix.

4. Spread some of the remaining olive oil in a non-stick skillet or frying pan and place on high heat.

   NOTE: You can also use a griddle if you have one.

5. Pour about ¼ cup of pancake mix onto the skillet once or twice (as will fit in the pan) and let cook.

6. Flip over when bubbles form on the surface and edges begin to dry.

7. Turn heat down to medium high and repeat steps 5 and 6 until all pancake mix has been used.

   NOTE: You will need to spread a little olive oil in the pan between sets of pancakes to keep them from sticking to the pan.

8. Serve with a small amount of honey or natural maple syrup.

Eggs in Different Styles

Breakfast eggs can be cooked in many different styles. In this recipe, we include how to cook eggs sunny side up, over easy, scrambled with zucchini and onions, and scrambled with mushrooms and onions.

The finished dishes

Ingredients:

For each type of egg dish:

4 eggs

1 Tbsp olive oil

¼ tsp salt

¼ tsp pepper

For scrambled eggs, also include:

2 oz of diced onions

½ zucchini, diced (4 oz)

OR

2 oz of mushrooms

2 oz diced tomatoes
   (optional)

EASY   ⊗

Preparation: 5 min.

Cooking time: 5 to 10 min.

Serves 2

Recipe:

To cook eggs sunny side up or over easy, do the following:

1. Spread olive oil in a non-stick skillet and place on medium heat. Let stand for one to two minutes.

Ingredients

2. Crack eggs in separate parts of the pan.

3. For eggs sunny side up, let them fry for 5 minutes, making sure the white of the egg is solid close to the yolk.

4. For eggs over easy, let them fry for about 3 minutes until the white and yolk of the eggs are hard before carefully flipping each egg over with a spatula. Cook on the other side for about 2 minutes.

Egg, sunny side up

5. Add salt and pepper, and serve (pict. 3).

To scramble eggs, either with zucchini and onions, or mushrooms and onions, do the following:

1. Spread olive oil in a non-stick skillet and place on medium heat. Let stand for 1 to 2 minutes.

Scrambled eggs with zucchini

2. Add the onions to the skillet and cook for 3 minutes while stirring constantly with a spatula.

3. Add the diced zucchini or mushrooms (or diced tomatoes, as an option) and cook for 2 minutes while stirring constantly.

4. Crack the eggs in the skillet on top of the ingredients, let cook for 1 minute, break the yolks and stir to mix with the ingredients, for 3 to 5 minutes, stirring periodically.

5. Remove from skillet and serve (pict. 4).

NOTE: You can also crack the eggs into a medium bowl and lightly beat before putting them in the skillet.

Oatmeal

For ease and convenience, we made this fast-cooking oatmeal from a package called Bob's Red Mill "Organic Quick Cooking Rolled Oats." It uses organic whole grain oats and nothing else. Look for it—or a similar product—at your local health food store, or order it online at www.bobsredmill.com. The recipe is a small variation from the instructions on the package.

To add flavor and texture, mix in soy milk and/or add raisins, berries or crushed nuts to taste. Dribble honey on top to sweeten.

The finished dish

Ingredients:

2 cups water

1 cup quick cooking
   organic whole grain oats

½ cup soy milk (optional)

3 Tbsp raisins (optional)

3 Tbsp walnuts (optional)

2 Tbsp honey

EASY

Preparation time: 10 min.
Cooking time: 6 min.
Serves 2

Recipe:

1. Bring water to a boil in medium pot on high heat.

2. Add oats from the package.

3. Cook for 4 minutes, stirring occasionally.

4. Remove from heat, cover and let stand for 2 minutes.

5. Stir in the following, to taste:
   - Soy milk
   - Raisins
   - Walnuts

6. Place in bowls to serve.

7. Dribble honey on top, and serve.

Ingredients

Rice and Grains

We've included a variety of tasty non-wheat dishes that truly satisfy, mostly using rice pasta and basmati rice, which is a lighter, fluffier and more aromatic rice. We encourage you to experiment, though, by substituting rice with other types of non-wheat grains, such as quinoa or millet. You can also try other types of rice. Keep in mind, though, that brown rice provides more nutrition than white, but white rice is less taxing on digestion.

In the recipes that follow, spices are used differently in each dish to bring out a variety of flavors, giving some dishes a hint of Italy and others a hint of Asia. Selected vegetables add both flavor and texture, and in one recipe, roasted pine nuts provide a crunchy feel that enlivens the dish.

Garlic Pasta

This quick-and-easy dish captures the flavor of southern Italy. This dish is meant to be eaten when cooked. It doesn't taste good after sitting in the refrigerator.

1

The finished dish

2

Ingredients

Ingredients:

10 oz of non-wheat
   spaghetti pasta (use
   quinoa or rice)

8 cloves of minced garlic

2 Tbsp olive oil

3 Tbsp water

¼ tsp salt

EASY

Preparation: 5 min.
Cooking time: 15 min.
Serves 2

Recipe:

1. Mice the garlic into small pieces and set aside.

2. Cook the pasta in a large pot with ¼ tsp of salt.
   - Bring about 2 quarts of water to a boil on high heat in a medium-size pot.
   - Add the pasta and cook for the exact time it says on the package (usually 7 to 10 minutes), stirring from time to time.
   - Drain the pasta and set aside.

3. Place 3 Tbsp of water in a small non-stick pot (pict. 3), add the chopped garlic and bring to a boil on high heat.

4. Turn heat down to medium and continue to boil for 5 minutes, until the garlic is soft.

5. Remove from heat, drain garlic from water and set aside.

6. Pour olive oil in a large non-stick skillet and place on medium heat.

7. Add garlic and cook for 2 minutes while moving around the pan (pict. 4). Be careful not to burn the garlic.

8. Add pasta to the pan with garlic and oil and mix well (pict. 5).

9. Serve.

Boiling garlic

Cooking boiled garlic

Adding pasta

Fried Rice

This dish is so flavorful and filling one could eat it non-stop. Fried in a small amount of healthy olive oil with a couple of eggs thrown in, it's Fertile Kitchen™'s take on a classic Chinese dish.

The finished dish

Ingredients

Ingredients:

1 cup of basmati rice

1 onion, diced

1 Tbsp of olive oil

2 eggs

1 zucchini

4 oz mushrooms

2 Tbsp wheat-free soy sauce

¼ tsp pepper

¼ tsp salt

EASY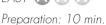

Preparation: 10 min.

Cooking time: 10 min.

Serves 4

Recipe:

1. Cook rice. (See recipe p.62 for *Fluffy Rice*.)

2. Put olive oil in a non-stick saucepan and place on medium heat.

3. Add diced onion and cook for 3 minutes while stirring regularly.

4. Add rice and stir well.

5. Add eggs and zucchini (pict. 3) and cook for 3 minutes, stirring every minute or so.

6. Add mushrooms, salt and pepper, stir well and cook for 3 more minutes.

7. Add soy sauce (pict. 4), mix and serve.

SUGGESTION: You can add or substitute any of the following ingredients: diced tomatoes, carrots, broccoli, bell pepper, chili, cilantro, basil, cooked meat or fish.

Adding eggs

Adding soy sauce

Fluffy Rice

Fluffy just means that it's not sticky. This basic and versatile food can be served with meat or main vegetable dishes, or used in other recipes, such as in the *Rice Salad* (see p.150).

1

The finished dish

2

Ingredients

Ingredients:

1 cup of basmati rice

1 and ½ cup water

¼ tsp salt

EASY

Preparation: 2 min.
Cooking time: 15 min.
Serves 2

Recipe:

1. Rinse rice in cold water 4 to 5 times until water drains clear. Use the pot you will cook the rice in to do that.

2. Add 1 and ¼ cups of water and ¼ tsp of salt to the pot with rice.

3. Place on the stove and bring to a boil on high heat.

4. Lower the heat to medium low so that it is barely simmering and cover.

   NOTE: When you cover the pot, leave a small opening to allow steam to escape.

5. Cook for 15 minutes or until all water is absorbed.

6. Remove from heat, fluff rice with a fork and place in serving dish.

NOTE: Do not cover again once cooked. This makes the rice stick.

TIP: If you want to keep the rice warm, place in the oven.

Pasta with Olives and Pine Nuts

This is a simple, colorful and tasty pasta.

1

The finished dish

2

Ingredients

Ingredients:

12 oz of rice pasta

3 to 4 oz of kalamata
   olives

½ cup of pine nuts

1 big tomato

1 yellow bell pepper

2 tsp olive oil

¼ tsp each of salt
   and pepper

¼ tsp salt

6 to 10 leaves of fresh
   basil, chopped

MEDIUM ⊗ ⊗ ⊗

Preparation time: 20 min.

Cooking time: 30 min.

Serves 4

Recipe:

1. Cut bell pepper and tomatoes in ¼-inch by ¼-inch pieces.

2. Chop basil leaves.

3. Cut olives in 2 or 4 pieces (remove the seed if applicable).

Roasting pine nuts

4. Put pine nuts in a non-stick skillet on medium heat with no oil.

5. Stir frequently to turn the nuts over and cook until the pine nuts start to become brown, which is about 5 minutes (pict. 3).

6. Set aside in a small bowl.

Adding tomatoes

7. Cook pasta with ¼ tsp salt according to instructions on the package so that it is al dente.

   - Bring about 2 cups of water to a boil on high heat in a medium pot.

   - Add pasta and salt, and cook for the exact time it says on the package so that it is al dente (usually 7 to 8 minutes), stirring from time to time.

Mixing in pasta

8. Drain pasta and rinse with cold water (to prevent further cooking) and set aside.

9. Add olive oil to the non-stick saucepan, heat on medium high, add bell pepper pieces and cook for 5 minutes.

10. Add tomatoes and cook for 3 more minutes (pict. 4).

11. Add salt, pepper and basil and mix well.

12. Add olives, pasta and pine nuts, mix well (pict. 5) and cook for 2 to 3 minutes more.

13. Place in a serving bowl.

SUGGESTION: You can also add zucchini and/or mushrooms at the same time as the tomatoes.

Light Mushroom Risotto

This dish is much lighter than classic risotto, yet still wonderfully flavorful. (Note: Arborio rice is typically used for risotto, but because of its high starch content, it should be avoided. Use basmati rice instead.

The finished dish

Ingredients

Ingredients:

1 small onion, diced

1 oz dry mushroom (porcini, morels, shiitake, or wild forest) or 4 to 6 oz of fresh mushrooms

1 cup of basmati rice (8 oz)

2 cup of water (16 fl oz)

1 cube of vegetable bouillon

2 Tbsp olive oil

EASY   ⊗

Preparation time: 10 min.
Cooking time: 20 min.
Serves 2

Recipe:

1. Soak mushrooms in a bowl of warm water for 15 to 30 minutes. Remove mushrooms and then press them to remove additional water.

2. Dice the onion.

3. Pour olive oil into a non-stick saucepan or pot and place on medium heat.

4. Add diced onions and cook for 5 minutes while stirring occasionally (pict. 3).

5. Add rice, mushrooms and bouillon cube (pict. 4).

6. Cook for 3 to 4 minutes, stirring frequently (pict. 5).

7. Add water (pict. 6), cover and cook for 15 to 20 minutes on low heat, until water appears to be absorbed.

   NOTE: If you use fresh mushrooms (4 to 6 oz), add those at the end of step 6.

Cooking onions

Adding rice and mushrooms

Stirring together

Adding water

Zucchini Pasta

This is a simple, light dish made with non-wheat pasta. (Rice pasta works best.)

1

The finished dish

2

Ingredients

Ingredients:

¾ lb of rice pasta (12 oz)

2 medium or 3 small
    zucchini

2 Tbsp of olive oil

2 x ¼ tsp of salt

¼ tsp pepper

2 tsp of dried basil or
    5 leaves of fresh basil,
    chopped

EASY

Preparation time: 5 min.
Cooking time: 15 min.
Serves 2

Recipe:

1. Cut both ends of zucchini off and peel every other side lengthwise (pict. 2) to reduce any bitterness.

2. Cut the zucchini lengthwise in 4, then into thin slices, about ⅛-inch thick (pict. 2).

3. Fill a large pot with 3 quarts of water, add ¼ tsp salt, and bring to a boil by cooking on high heat.

4. Add pasta and cook for 7 to 10 minutes, depending on cooking instructions written on pasta package.

5. Pour olive oil into a non-stick skillet and place on medium to low heat.

6. Add zucchini (pict. 3) and cook for 5 minutes, stirring well.

7. Add remaining salt, pepper and basil, and mix well (pict. 4).

8. Drain pasta when it's ready.

9. Add pasta into the skillet and mix well (pict. 5).

10. Serve.

Adding zucchini

Adding spices

Mixing in pasta

Pizza a la Polenta

Although this looks like a pizza, it tastes nothing like it. It's a hearty meal of polenta with chicken, flavored with tomatoes and basil.

The finished dish

Ingredients:

1 cup of polenta
  (corn semolina)

4 cups of water

1 tsp salt

¼ tsp pepper
  (freshly ground is best)

2 tomatoes

6 to 8 leaves of fresh
  basil, chopped

2 chicken tenderloins
  (or 1 chicken breast)

2 tsp olive oil

EASY ⊗ ⊗ ⊗

Preparation time: 15 min.

Cooking time: 75 min.

Serves 6

Recipe:

1. Bring water to a boil on high heat in a large pot (pict. 3).

2. Add salt and pour in the corn semolina slowly, mixing well.

3. Lower heat to medium, cover and cook for 30 minutes, stirring every 5 minutes or so.

4. Remove from stove, stir and let cool down for 15 minutes.

5. Pour polenta into an oiled baking sheet to create "pizzas" of approximately 5 inches in diameter (pict. 4). You may need a second baking sheet to use all of the polenta.

6. Spread the polenta so that it's thin (about ¼-inch thick).

7. Cut basil leaves into 4 or 5 pieces and also place on top of polenta.

8. Slice tomatoes and place them atop the polenta and basil, as you would on a pizza. Cover basil so it will not burn in the oven.

9. Use scissors to cut raw chicken into small pieces and place them on polenta.

10. Add pepper.

11. Preheat the oven at 450°F and cook for 30 minutes.

    NOTE: The thinner or smaller round the polenta, the faster it will cook.

12. Use a spatula to remove from the baking sheet.

    SUGGESTIONS: You can also:
    - Replace chicken and basil with anchovies, olives and capers.
    - Add olive oil before putting into the oven.
    - Add an egg on top 5 minutes before removing from the oven.

    NOTE: These are as good cold as they are warm.

Ingredients

Boiling corn semolina

Pouring polenta into the pan

Mixed Rice and Vegetables

Light, healthy and colorful.

1

The finished dish

2

Ingredients

Ingredients:

1 cup of basmati rice

1 and ½ cup water

¼ tsp salt

½ carrot

½ yellow bell pepper
   (or 3 baby bell peppers)

1 small zucchini

EASY

Preparation time: 10 min.
Cooking time: 25 min.
Serves 2

Recipe:

1. Cut carrot in half lengthwise, then in half again.

2. Cut carrot again in ¼- to ⅛-inch pieces.

3. Cut zucchini like the carrot.

4. Cut bell pepper into ¼- x ¼- inch thick pieces.

5. Rinse rice in cold water 4 to 5 times until the water drains clean.

6. Put rice in a medium pot.

7. Add 1 and ½ cup of water and ¼ tsp salt, cover and bring to a boil on high heat (picts. 3 and 4).

8. Lower heat and leave a small opening in the cover for the steam to escape.

9. Add chopped bell pepper after 4 minutes.

10. Add carrot pieces after 4 more minutes.

11. Add zucchini after 2 more minutes.

12. Cook until water is absorbed, approximately 10 minutes (pict. 5).

13. Remove from heat, fluff the rice with a fork and serve.

   NOTE: Do not cover the rice once cooked or it will stick.

   TIP: If you need to reheat the rice, put it in the oven.

Cooking rice

Covering

Cooking mixture until water is absorbed

Crêpes Salées

It is hard to believe these light and tasty crêpes contain no wheat. As this version is meant to be eaten with non-sweet fillings, you can get creative with what you stuff in them. Ours is shown with *Sautéed Mushrooms in Lemon Juice* (see recipe p.80).

The finished dish with sautéed mushrooms

Ingredients

Ingredients:

1 cup of rice flour (or 7 oz)

4 eggs

¾ cup unsweetened soy milk

¾ cup water

½ tsp salt

2 tsp olive oil

EASY ⊗ ⊗ ⊗

Preparation time: 15 min.
Cooking time: 15 min.
Serves 4 (8 crêpes)

Recipe:

1. Put rice flour in a large mixing bowl.

2. Add salt, soy milk and water and mix well.

3. Add eggs and beat mixture until it has a uniform consistency (pict. 3).

4. Cover and let stand for 10 to 15 minutes.

5. Mix batter well with a spoon or ladle, as flour will have deposited to the bottom of the bowl.

6. Put ¼ tsp of oil in a non-stick skillet and place on medium high heat. Wait a minute or so for the pan to heat up for the first crêpe.

7. Add about 1 cup of batter to the skillet, tilting the skillet in all directions to spread the batter across its bottom surface (pict. 4).

8. Cook for 4 to 5 minutes until batter appears solid (pict. 5).

9. Flip the crêpe over and cook the other side for 3 to 4 minutes (pict. 6), remove from pan and set aside.

   TIP: To tell if the crêpe is ready to flip, use a spatula to see if it no longer sticks to the pan and is a little stiff. You can also peek under to see that the color has started to turn slightly brown.

   NOTES: If the batter bubbles, the heat is too high; lower the heat. Be careful not to leave the skillet on the hot burner with nothing in it (between crêpes); this will cause the skillet to overheat and potentially burn the crêpe. It also damages the skillet.

(continued on next page)

Beating in eggs

Spreading batter in pan

Ready to turn over

Cooking the other side

Adding mushroom filling

10. Add ¼ tsp oil to the skillet and repeat steps 7 to 10 until the batter is finished.

11. Add a mushroom filling to each crêpe (pict. 7), fold twice over, and serve. For this filling, see the recipe p.80 for *Sautéed Mushrooms in Lemon Juice.*

SUGGESTIONS: You can also serve these crêpes with *Ground Turkey Mix* (see recipe p.122) or *Sautéed Spinach* (see recipe p.92), or any other favorite, non-sweet filling. Be sure to drain as much liquid from any filling before use.

NOTE: For crêpes to be used with fruits and other sweet fillings, see *Crêpes Sucrées* recipe p.176.

Vegetables

Feel free to go wild on vegetables and eat as much as you want of them! Besides being rich in vitamins, antioxidants and other healthy nutrients, vegetables taste good! Our recipes include a diverse array of vegetables, many of them sautéed with garlic, onions and/or spices to enhance the vegetable's original flavors. Our Stuffed Vegetables *dish makes for great comfort food, while our* Carrots with Garlic and Cilantro *delivers sweetness with a fresh, crisp bite. Also check out our* Schezwan Green Beans *and* Roasted Baby Bell Peppers. *Remember to use organic produce in all the recipes.*

Sautéed Leeks

These leeks work well as a healthy side dish, but even better, is to mix them into something else for more flavor and texture. Cindy prefers to add them to lentils or rice.

1

The finished dish

2

Ingredients

Ingredients:

1 ½ lbs of leeks

¼ tsp salt

⅛ tsp pepper

2 Tbsp olive oil

EASY ✖ ✖ ✖

Preparation time: 15 min.

Cooking time: 15 min.

Serves 4

Recipe:

1. Remove any old or damaged leaves.

2. Cut off the ends of green leaves (1 to 2 inches) and tip of the bulbs off.

3. Cut leeks into ¼- to ⅛-inch sections.

4. Clean with water and drain 2 or 3 times (pict. 3).

5. Put olive oil in a saucepan and place on medium heat.

6. Add leeks, salt and pepper, and mix well (pict. 4).

7. Cover and cook for 10 minutes (picts. 5 and 6).

   NOTE: If you are not using a non-stick pan or the cover is not a good fit, you may need to add ½ a cup of water to ensure the leeks do not get stuck on the bottom of the pan.

8. Drain if needed and serve.

Cleaning leeks

Adding leeks to pan

Covering pan

All done

Sautéed Mushrooms in Lemon Juice

This light dish is perfect for stuffing into crêpes (see *Crêpes Salées*, p.74), or serving on the side of chicken or rice.

The finished dish

Ingredients

Ingredients:

1 lb fresh mushrooms (baby bella, white or cremini mushrooms)

½ onion, diced

2 Tbsp olive oil

¼ tsp salt

⅛ tsp black pepper

7 leaves of fresh basil, chopped

½ lemon juice (1 Tbsp)

EASY   ✗

Preparation time: 10 min.

Cooking time: 10 min.

Serves 4

Recipe:

1. Slice mushrooms in 4 pieces and place in a medium bowl. (You don't need to cut chanterelles, as they are small enough.)

2. Add lemon juice to the mushrooms.

3. Chop basil leaves into small pieces and add to the mushrooms.

4. Dice the onion and place in a non-stick saucepan or skillet with the olive oil on medium heat, stirring frequently.

5. Cook for 5 minutes.

6. Add bowl of mushrooms, basil and lemon juice to the saucepan and mix well (picts. 3 and 4).

7. Cover and cook for 5 minutes (pict. 5).

8. Remove lid and cook on medium heat until liquid is mostly evaporated for about 2 to 3 minutes (pict. 6).

9. Serve.

SUGGESTIONS: Lemon gives this dish a light, zesty flavor. You can also try the recipe without it, or with only ¼ lemon juice, for less "zest."

You can use 3 shallots instead of ½ onion, which gives a "smoother" flavor.

Adding mushroom mix

Stirring it in with onions

Covering

Evaporating excess liquid

Mixed Vegetables

This is a healthy, colorful, flavorful dish that tastes great on its own, or you can use it as a side dish.

The finished dish

Ingredients:

1 yellow bell pepper

1 red bell pepper

3 zucchini

1 small onion, sliced

10 baby carrots

2 heads of broccoli florets

5 oz of fresh sliced
    mushroom

¼ tsp salt

¼ tsp pepper

¼ tsp thyme

8 basil leaves

2 Tbsp olive oil

1 Tbsp water

EASY

Preparation time: 15 min.

Cooking time: 15 min.

Serves 4

Recipe:

1. Cut and prepare vegetables: cut mushrooms into medium, thin slices, cut zucchini into ¼-inch cylinder slices, cut bell peppers and onions into medium-thin slices, and cut broccoli into smaller pieces.

2. Spread olive oil on a non-stick saucepan and place on medium heat.

3. Add sliced onion and cook for 2 minutes while stirring (pict. 2).

4. Add bell pepper and cook for 3 minutes while stirring (pict. 3).

5. Add carrots, broccoli and spices, mix in and cover (pict. 4).

6. Cook for 5 minutes.

7. Add zucchini, mushroom and 1 Tbsp water (pict. 5). Make sure there is always a little liquid in the pan or it will burn.

8. Stir, cover and cook for 3 minutes.

9. Serve.

Cooking onions

Adding bell peppers

Covering

Adding zucchini and mushrooms

Roasted Baby Bell Peppers

These colorful baby bell peppers look like jalapeños, but they're not. They're sweet and loaded with vitamin C and A. They also make for a great side dish, served hot or cold.

The finished dish

Ingredients

Ingredients:

10 to 15 baby
    bell peppers
2 Tbsp olive oil

EASY

Preparation time: 5 min.
Cooking time: 20 min.
Serves 2 to 4

Recipe:

1. Preheat the oven to 425°F.

2. Place baby bell peppers in an oven dish.

3. Add olive oil and mix well, making sure baby bell peppers are fully coated in oil. (pict. 3)

Ready to go in the oven

4. Place in the oven for 20 minutes.

5. Remove and serve. Can also be put in the refrigerator and served chilled.

NOTE: If you use regular bell peppers instead, you will first need to peel them to remove the bitterness. Cut each bell pepper in 4 and remove seeds. To peal them, put them in the oven for 10 to 15 minutes without putting oil on the skin. The skin will burn/blister. Remove the bell peppers from the oven, put in a plastic bag until cool and peel. Cut them in slices and add olive oil. Put in the refrigerator and serve when chilled, or put them back in the oven for 5 minutes to warm them up.

TIP: You can also roast baby bell peppers on the barbeque. Do not put them directly on the heat, as this will burn the skin. Keep them off to the side of the main heat and turn them after 5 to 10 minutes.

Stuffed Vegetables

Bell peppers, tomatoes and eggplants stuffed with delicious ground turkey —and it goes great with rice.

The finished dish

Ingredients:

1 eggplant

1 bell pepper

2 tomatoes

3 lbs ground turkey

15 oz diced tomatoes

3 small onions, diced

8 oz fresh mushroom, sliced

2 Tbsp olive oil

½ tsp dry basil

¼ tsp thyme

¼ tsp salt

¼ tsp pepper

3 bay leaves

1 vegetable bouillon cube

1 tsp paprika

1 tsp Italian herbs*

* See Spices on p.43.

MEDIUM

Preparation time: 45 min.

Cooking time: 45 min.

Serves 4

Recipe:

1. Cut the middle out of the vegetables (bell pepper, tomatoes and eggplant) (pict. 6).

2. Cook diced onions in olive oil for 5 minutes on medium heat (pict. 2).

3. Add ground turkey meat (pict. 3) and cook on high for 5 minutes while mixing.

4. Add spices and bouillon cube and mix well.

5. Add tomatoes, carved portion of the vegetables and mix well (pict. 4).

6. Lower heat to medium, cover (pict. 5) and let cook for 20 minutes.

7. Add sliced mushrooms, stir and remove from heat.

8. Fill vegetables with meat stuffing and place in a large Pyrex dish or deep cookie sheet.

9. Set the oven to 425°F, put in the oven for 20 minutes.

10. Serve.

Cooking onions

Adding ground turkey

Adding tomatoes and mixing

Covering

Hallowing vegetables

Steamed Vegetables

Steaming vegetables retains more nutrients than if you cook them any other way. They're healthy, light and make a great side dish. You ideally want steamed vegetables slightly crunchy and not overdone. This recipe covers steaming asparagus, cauliflower, broccoli and zucchini—all meant to be cooked individually and served separately.

1

The finished dish

2

Ingredients

Ingredients:

20 asparagus (1 bunch)

1 head of cauliflower

3 large broccoli florets

4 zucchini

EASY

Preparation time: 10 min.
for each vegetable
Cooking time: 2 to 5 min.

Recipe:

1. Prepare vegetable you'd like to steam.
   If asparagus, leave as is, or cut just hard ends off (leave the tips).
   If cauliflower or broccoli, cut into small pieces.
   If zucchini, cut into ¼-to ½-inch thick round pieces.

2. Add 1 inch of water to a large pot, cover and bring to a boil.

3. Put vegetable you are cooking in the pot and cover (picts. 3 and 4).

   NOTE: You can also use a steamer. Place vegetable in basket (or grid) after water boils (picts. 5 and 6).

4. Let cook for a time period as listed below.

Asparagus:	3 minutes
Cauliflower:	5 minutes
Broccoli:	3 minutes
Zucchini:	2 minutes

5. Remove from the pot immediately and place in a serving dish.

   NOTE: Timing is very important. If you do not remove from the pot immediately, the vegetables may become overcooked and too soft.

   Cooking times may vary slightly depending on the size of the pot, how the lid seals and the type of stove you use. You can also sample a vegetable for readiness.

Asparagus

Broccoli

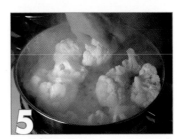
Cauliflower

Zucchini

Schezwan Green Beans

This lively, original side dish breaks the monotony of plain, steamed green beans and fills your palate with flavor.

The finished dish

Ingredients

Ingredients:

1 lb of green beans

6 garlic cloves, sliced

1-inch long piece of ginger, sliced

3 Tbsp of wheat-free soy sauce

1 Tbsp olive oil

EASY   ⊗

Preparation time: 10 min.
Cooking time: 15 min.
Serves 2

Recipe:

1. Cut both tips of the green beans and then rinse, or use frozen, prepared green beans.

2. Cut garlic into thin slices.

3. Peel and cut ginger into thick slices.

4. Spread olive oil into a non-stick saucepan and place on high heat.

5. Add green beans, garlic and ginger.

6. Cook for 3 minutes while stirring.

7. Lower heat to medium, add soy sauce (pict. 3), and stir for 1 minute.

8. Cover (pict. 4) and let simmer for 5 to 7 minutes. (Add 1 Tbsp water before covering if there appears to be no more liquid in the pan.)

9. Taste green beans for readiness (tender, but still crunchy) and simmer for 1 to 2 minutes more if needed.

10. Remove cover, increase heat to high, and stir until all liquid is evaporated (pict. 5).

11. Serve.

Adding soy sauce

Covering

Final stirring

Sautéed Spinach

This is a rich, flavorful, healthy side dish that goes well with rice.

The finished dish

Ingredients:

1 lb fresh spinach*

½ large onion, diced

3 garlic cloves, minced

1 tsp of vegetable broth

¼ tsp salt

¼ tsp pepper

¼ tsp of nutmeg

2 Tbsp of olive oil

*TIP: You can also use packaged organic spinach leaves, which shortens preparation time by 5 minutes.

EASY ⊗ ⊗ ⊗

Preparation time: 10 min.

Cooking time: 10 min.

Serves 2

Recipe:

1. Cut spinach about 1 inch away from where the stems join.

2. Clean spinach several times, until the water is clear and free of dirt.

3. Dice onion, mince the garlic.

4. Put oil into a deep non-stick pot and place on medium heat, add diced onion, and cook for 5 minutes, stirring frequently.

5. Add in as much spinach as will fit in the pot (pict. 3), and cover. Let stand for about 30 seconds and then mix and add more spinach. Repeat this step until all the spinach is in the pot.

6. Add minced garlic, vegetable broth, salt, pepper and nutmeg (pict. 4).

7. Mix well, cover and cook for 5 minutes, stirring regularly throughout.

8. When finished, drain liquid and place in a dish to serve.

Ingredients

Adding spinach

Adding spices

Sautéed Fennel

This quick vegetable side dish is both mildly crunchy (in the fennels) and creamy (with the onions).

1

The finished dish

2

Ingredients

Ingredients:

2 fennel bulbs

¼ onion, diced

1 Tbsp olive oil

¼ tsp salt

¼ tsp pepper

½ cup water

EASY ✖ ✖ ✖

Preparation time: 5 min.

Cooking time: 20 min.

Serves 2

Recipe:

1. Dice the onion and set aside.

2. Cut feathery leaves off fennel and also cut off the bottom of fennel bulbs (pict. 3).

3. Cut each bulb lengthwise into 3 pieces (pict. 3).

4. Put olive oil and diced onion into a skillet and cook on medium heat for 3 minutes, stirring 3 or 4 times (pict. 4).

5. Add chopped fennel bulbs, salt, pepper, water and stir a few times.

6. Cover and cook on medium heat for 15 minutes (pict. 5).

7. Serve.

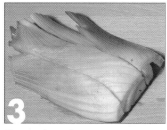

Cutting fennel

Cooking onions

Covering fennel

Sautéed Bok Choy

This is a great, healthy light side dish, and easy-to-make.

The finished dish

Ingredients

Ingredients:
1 ½ lbs bok choy
½ large onion, diced
¼ tsp each of salt
    and pepper
2 Tbsp olive oil

EASY ⊗ ⊗ ⊗
Preparation time: 5 min.
Cooking time: 10 min.
Serves 4

Recipe:

1. Cut bok choy in ½-inch slices (pict. 3).

2. Place diced onion and oil in a non-stick skillet on medium heat.

3. Cook for 5 minutes.

4. Add bok choy, salt and pepper, and cover (pict. 4).

5. Cook for 5 minutes.

6. Serve.

   TIP: This bok choy dish works well with soy sauce on the side.

Preparing bok choy

Cooking and covering

Carrots with Garlic and Cilantro

This is Cindy's favorite of Pierre's vegetable dishes! The cilantro makes this sweet dish fresh and tasty.

The finished dish

Ingredients

Ingredients:

6 big carrots (1.5 lbs)

4 cloves of garlic

½ bunch of fresh cilantro

¼ tsp each of salt
    and pepper

2 x ½ cup of water

EASY   ⊗

Preparation time: 10 min.

Cooking time: 10 min.

Serves 4

Recipe:

1. Brush carrots clean and cut off bases and tip of each carrot.

2. Slice carrots into ¼- to ⅛-inch thick rounds.

3. Remove germ of garlic and slice it into small pieces (as seen in pict. 4).

4. Remove stems of cilantro and cut leaves only into small pieces (pict. 3).

5. Place sliced carrots and garlic in a non-stick skillet with a ½ cup of water, cover and bring to a boil on high heat (pict. 4).

   NOTE: If the cover is not a good fit, you may need to add more water or carrots may burn.

6. Reduce to medium high heat and boil for 5 minutes, making sure there is always a little water in the pan and add a little if needed.

7. Add salt, pepper, cilantro and mix.

8. Add another ¼ cup of water.

9. Boil for another 3 minutes (pict. 5), and again make sure there is always a little water in pan and add a little if needed.

10. Drain if needed and serve.

Cutting cilantro

Cooking carrots

Almost ready

BBQ Marinated Asparagus

Asparagus is a wonderful vegetable for the barbeque, resulting in a dish that's flavorful and crunchy. In addition, asparagus contains plenty of folate, an important B vitamin that helps boost fertility and prevent birth defects. A barbeque is not required. You can also use the oven.

The finished dish

Ingredients

Ingredients:

1 lb green asparagus

2 Tbsp olive oil

1 Tbsp dry basil

1 Tbsp dry Italian herbs*

2 garlic cloves, minced

* See "Spices" on p.43.

EASY

Preparation time: 10 min.
Cooking time: 5 min.
Serves 4

Recipe:

1. Cut off bottom ends of asparagus (yellow or hard portion).

2. Put asparagus in a glass or Tupperware container.

3. Add olive oil, herbs and minced garlic to container, mixing well and spreading all over asparagus (pict. 3).

4. Let stand for 2 or more hours (overnight is okay).

5. Light barbeque and let it warm up.

   NOTE: You can also cook in the oven at 400°F for 10 minutes in a Pyrex dish (pre-heat first).

6. Put asparagus away from the fire and close the lid of barbeque.

7. Cook for 3 minutes and then turn over.

8. Cook another 2 to 3 minutes.

9. Remove from heat and serve.

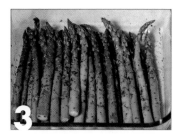

Asparagus in a dish

Beans and Other Legumes

Have you ever had a healthy, light version of chili con carne that tasted just as rich and fulfilling as the original? We've got the recipe here, along with one for mildly spicy garbanzo beans and a couple of traditional, yet more savory bean recipes.

Don't be shy about eating beans! Not only are they packed with protein, fiber and important nutrients, but they also contain a high percentage of folate, which boosts fertility in both men and women and helps prevent certain birth defects. Remember to avoid peas, though, which contain a natural contraceptive (m-xylohydroquinine).

Chili con Carne

This healthy version of chili con carne still makes for a warm, hearty dish. Perfect comfort food!

The finished dish

Ingredients:

1.5 lbs ground turkey

1 10 oz can of cooked pinto beans

1 Tbsp olive oil

1 onion, diced

4 garlic cloves, minced

¼ tsp cumin

1 tsp chili pepper

1 Tbsp paprika

3 bay leaves

½ Serrano pepper

¼ tsp salt and pepper

2 vegetable bouillon cubes

6 fl oz hot water

2 tsp rice flour

MEDIUM

Preparation time: 15 min.

Cooking time: 45 min.

Serves 4

Recipe:

1. Dice onion into small pieces and mince garlic.

2. Put olive oil in a deep saucepan and place on medium heat.

3. Add diced onion and cook for 2 minutes, stirring regularly.

4. Add ground meat (pict. 3), increase heat to high, and cook for 10 minutes, stirring every minute or so. Watch carefully to make sure the meat doesn't burn (pict. 4).

5. Add bay leaves, paprika, cumin, chili pepper, Serrano pepper, minced garlic, salt, pepper, bouillon cube and hot water.

6. Mix well and cook for 3 minutes while stirring (pict 5).

7. Lower heat to medium and cook covered for another 15 minutes.

8. Rinse pinto beans with cold water in a colander.

9. Add beans to the ground meat, mix well and cook another 5 minutes.

10. In a separate bowl, mix in 2 Tbsp of hot water and 2 tsp of rice flour. Add this mixture to the ground meat and mix well. This thickens the chili.

11. Remove bay leaves and serve.

    TIP: You can replace pinto beans with black beans, and ground turkey with organic ground beef.

Ingredients

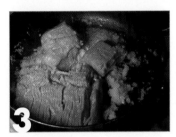
Adding meat

Cooking meat

Almost done

Lentils with Onions

Lentils are high in protein, fiber and rich nutrients. This rich, flavorful dish can be served on rice as a main dish, on the side, or even tossed into salads.

The finished dish

Ingredients

Ingredients:

1 cup of French lentils
(7 oz)

2 Tbsp olive oil

½ onion, diced

1 bouillon cube

2 to 2 and ½ cup of water

¼ tsp salt

¼ tsp pepper

EASY

Preparation time: 5 min.

Cooking time: 40 min.

Serves 2

Recipe:

1. Rinse lentils thoroughly. (They sometimes contain small stones which need to be removed.)

2. Put olive oil in a saucepan and place on medium high heat. Wait a minute or so for the pan to heat up.

3. Add diced onions and cook for 5 minutes, stirring regularly (pict. 3).

4. Add lentils, salt, pepper, bouillon cube and water (pict. 4).

5. Stir, cover and lower heat to medium.

6. Cook for 30 to 40 minutes, until all water is absorbed (pict. 5).

7. Serve, or let cool and toss onto a salad.

   NOTE: You can also use other kinds of lentils, but green French lentils are the finest and stay firm even when cooked. Other kinds of lentils will cook faster.

Cooking onions

Adding bouillon cube and water

Ready: water is absorbed

Spicy Garbanzo Beans

Full of protein, this flavorful dish can be served on the side or as an appetizer, both warm and cold. It's also fast and easy-to-make.

The finished dish

Ingredients

Ingredients:

1 10 oz can of cooked
    garbanzo beans, drained

1 onion, diced

4 garlic cloves, minced

1 tsp turmeric

1 tsp paprika

¼ tsp pepper

¼ tsp salt

2 Tbsp olive oil

EASY

Preparation time: 10 min.
Cooking time: 10 min.
Serves 2

Recipe:

1. Place olive oil in a pot, add diced onion and cook on medium high heat for 5 minutes (pict. 3), stirring regularly.

2. Add minced garlic and spices and mix well (pict. 4).

3. Add garbanzo beans and cook for 5 minutes (pict. 5).

   TIP: You can use curry or cayenne pepper for a stronger flavor.

   NOTE: If you work from dry beans (as opposed to those from a can), be sure to remove stones or damaged beans first, and soak beans overnight in cold water in the fridge before cooking. Soaking will remove the "bad" agent and prevent flatulence. Cook in boiling water for 1 to 2 hours (until soft). Drain and rinse.

Cooking onions

Adding spices

Adding garbanzo beans

Black Beans

Black beans are packed with fiber, antioxidants and nutrition. You can serve them hot over rice, or cold as a salad or snack.

The finished dish

Ingredients

Ingredients:

1 10 oz can of cooked
   black beans, drained

1 Tbsp olive oil

1 small onion (3 oz), diced

4 garlic cloves, minced

⅛ tsp salt

⅛ tsp pepper

¹⁄₁₆ tsp cayenne pepper

EASY

Preparation time: 10 min.

Cooking time: 10 min.

Serves 4

Recipe:

1. Drain cooked beans from their water, rinse well using a colander and set aside.

   NOTE: If you work from dry beans (as opposed to those from a can), be sure to remove stones or damaged beans first, and then soak beans overnight in cold water in fridge before cooking. Soaking will remove "bad" agent and prevent flatulence. Cook in boiling water for 1 to 2 hours (until soft). Drain and rinse.

2. Pour olive oil into a medium non-stick pot (or saucepan) and place on medium heat.

3. Add diced onion and cook for 3 minutes while stirring frequently.

4. Add the minced garlic and cayenne pepper, mix well and cook for 3 minutes (pict. 3).

5. Add beans, salt and pepper, cook for 3 minutes on medium high heat while stirring (pict. 4).

6. Serve over rice or with crackers, hot or cold.

   SUGGESTIONS: You can also make the following modifications:

   - Add ⅛ tsp cumin with the salt and pepper to remove sweetness.

   - If you serve it cold as a bean salad, you can also add a chopped, uncooked onion at the end.

   - Add in some cooked chicken or beef, cut in very small pieces.

   - Add in some diced tomatoes.

Adding spices

Adding black beans

Recipes

Meat and Poultry

We've included a variety of appetizing main dishes in this section. One of our favorites includes Lamb Curry in Coconut Milk, *with its rich ethnic flavors and melt-in-your-mouth tender lamb.* Chicken en Papillotes *also delivers a delectable, uncommonly moist chicken under the flow of a rich-tasting mushroom sauce. Our Asian-inspired* Chicken and Broccoli Rice Noodles *is light and flavorful.*

Keep in mind that red meat is good for building blood, but should be eaten in moderation. Remember to eat only organic meat and poultry, and only lean portions.

Chicken in Tomato Sauce

This is a great dish to serve with pasta or rice, or even by itself.

The finished dish

Ingredients:

6 pieces of chicken breast
    tenderloins (or 2 chicken
    breasts), about 12 to
    16 oz

¼ diced onion

1 28 oz can of diced
    tomatoes (you can
    also use 4 fresh
    tomatoes, diced)

2 Tbsp olive oil

¼ tsp each of salt
    and pepper

1 Tbsp vegetable broth

2 tsp dry basil or 3 to 4
    leaves of fresh basil,
    chopped

½ tsp dry thyme

EASY
Preparation time: 10 min.
Cooking time: 15 min.
Serves 2 to 4

Ingredients

Recipe:

1. Pour olive oil into a non-stick skillet or saucepan.

2. Add diced onion and cook on medium heat for 5 minutes, stirring continuously, until onions are transparent. Be careful not to burn onions by keeping the temperature not too high.

Adding tomatoes and spices

3. Add diced tomatoes, thyme and vegetable broth to the pan. Cook for 7 minutes on medium high heat (pict. 3).

4. Pull tomatoes to the sides of the pan, add cut chicken tenderloins into center (pict. 4), and then add salt, pepper and basil (pict. 5).

Adding chicken

5. Cook for 3 minutes, turn chicken over and let cook for another 3 minutes.

   NOTE: If you're using whole chicken breasts, cook for 5 minutes, turn over, and cook for an additional 5 minutes.

6. Mix well and cook another 2 minutes (pict. 6).

7. Serve.

Adding more spices

After mixing

Lamb Stew

This rich, savory dish is a variation on the *Lamb Curry in Coconut Milk* (recipe, p.120) and makes for great comfort food with rice or steamed potatoes. The slow, long cooking time ensures the lamb is tender.

The finished dish

Ingredients:

2+ lbs lean lamb meat

2 large onions, diced

3 carrots

3 garlic cloves, minced

4 tomatoes, diced or
    1 14 oz can of diced
    tomatoes

½ cup olive oil

4 bay leaves

¼ tsp each salt and pepper

4 garlic cloves, minced

1 Tbsp dry vegetable
    bouillon (or 1 cube)

½ tsp Herbs de Provence*

3 cloves

* See "Spices" on p.43.

MEDIUM

Preparation time: 15 min., 45 if meat needs to be trimmed of fat

Cooking time: 30 min. + 2 hours

Serves 6

Ingredients

Recipe:

1. Cut lamb into ½- to 1-inch cubes.

2. Dice onions and mince garlic.

3. Cut carrots into sections of 1 inch, and cut those in half.

4. Pour olive oil into a medium non-stick pot and place on high heat.

Sautéing lamb

5. Add lamb and sauté it until brown, about 10 to 15 minutes (pict. 3). NOTE: During the first 5 to 7 minutes, the meat may release some liquid.

6. Remove about ½ the oil from pot, leaving meat in the pan. (This is around ¼ cup of oil.)

Adding onions

7. Add onions to pot, mix well and cook for about 5 to 7 minutes (pict. 4).

8. Add, salt, pepper, garlic, Herbs de Provence and cook for 2 minutes more while stirring (pict. 5).

9. Add diced tomatoes (pict. 6), bouillon, bay leaves and cloves, stirring a couple of times. When it simmers, reduce heat to low.

10. Cover and simmer for 1 hour.

11. Add carrots and let cook for 20 more minutes, covered.

12. Serve with rice or steamed potatoes.

Adding tomatoes

Adding spices

Lamb Roast

This recipe makes for a hearty main dish. You can also serve leftovers cold in a salad, sandwich or fried rice dish. Like all meats, make sure the lamb is all natural with no additives, preservatives, growth hormones or antibiotics. Organic is best.

The finished dish

Ingredients:

Lamb shoulder
   (about 3 to 4 lbs)
4 carrots
2 tomatoes
10 small potatoes
1 onion, cut
5 garlic cloves,
   cut or crushed

2 Tbsp of mustard
½ tsp salt
½ tsp pepper
2 to 3 branches of
   rosemary

MEDIUM ✖ ✖ ✖
Preparation time: 15 min.
Cooking time: 60 min.
Serves 4

Recipe:

1. Preheat the oven to 450°F.

2. Cut 4 of the garlic cloves in 2, crush the last clove.

3. Cut 8 holes, 1-inch deep, in meat and place garlic inside.

4. In a separate bowl, mix mustard, salt, pepper, crushed garlic and rosemary.

5. Rub all sides of meat with mustard mixture.

6. Put roast in an oven dish. Place 1 branch of rosemary on the side.

7. Cut 2 of the carrots in half, the onion in 4 pieces and tomatoes in 4 pieces.

8. Add cut carrots, onion and tomatoes, plus 2 to 3 potatoes, in the dish to the side of the meat (pict. 3).

9. Put the roast in the oven for 40 minutes.

10. Add 2 more carrots, both cut in half, plus 6 to 10 potatoes to dish.

11. Cook for another 20 minutes, and then serve (pict. 4).

    NOTE: If serving cold from leftovers, note that the fat in the juices will congeal in the refrigerator, making it easy to remove unwanted fat from its surface.

Ingredients

Ready to go in the oven

Coming out of the oven

Lamb Curry in Coconut Milk

This is a great curry meal. The coconut milk makes the dish lighter, and the slow, long cooking ensures the lamb is tender and tasty. It is easy to prepare this dish in large quantities for entertainment or freezing.

The finished dish

Ingredients:

2+ lbs lean lamb meat

1 lb celery

2 large onions, diced

1 bunch of green onions

3 garlic cloves, minced

1 14 oz can of coconut milk

½ cup olive oil

2 tsp curry powder

⅛ tsp cayenne pepper

1 tsp paprika

¼ tsp each of salt and pepper

2 tsp turmeric

4 bay leaves

MEDIUM

Preparation time: 15 min., 45 if meat needs to be trimmed of fat

Cooking time: 30 min. + 2 hours

Serves 6

Recipe:

1. Cut lamb into ½- to 1-inch cubes (pict. 2).

2. Cut celery into ¼-inch slices.

3. Dice onions and mince garlic.

4. Cut green onions into 1-inch long sections.

5. Pour olive oil into a non-stick saucepan and place on high heat.

6. Add lamb and sauté until brown, about 10 to 15 minutes (pict. 3). Note that during the first 5 to 7 minutes the meat may release some liquid.

7. Transfer meat to a crock pot* using a slotted spoon, which leaves the oil in the saucepan.

8. Remove ½ the oil from saucepan and lower heat to medium high.

9. Add onions to saucepan and sauté them until translucent for about 5 to 7 minutes (pict. 4).

10. Add celery, cayenne, salt, pepper and green onions to saucepan and sauté for 3 minutes.

11. Add garlic, curry, turmeric and paprika and sauté for 2 minutes more (pict. 5).

12. Add coconut milk and stir a couple of times until the sauce starts to bubble (but doesn't boil) (pict. 6).

13. Transfer sauce in the saucepan to crock pot, add bay leaves, stir and cook in crock pot on high heat for 1 hour.

14. Reduce to low heat on the crock pot and cook for 2 more hours.

15. Serve with rice.

    *NOTE: You can cook the entire dish in saucepan if you don't have a crock pot. Just skip step 7 and 13 and simmer for 2 to 3 hours in covered pan.

Ingredients

Browning meat

Sautéing onions

Adding spices

Stirring in coconut milk

Ground Turkey Mix

This dish makes for an excellent pasta sauce. You can also serve it with rice.
The carrots make the dish mildly sweet.

The finished dish

Ingredients:

1 lb of ground turkey meat

1 large onion, diced

3 carrots

8 diced tomatoes or
   1 28 oz can of diced
   tomatoes

4 garlic cloves, minced

2 Tbsp of olive oil

1 Tbsp Italian herbs*

2 Tbsp of dry vegetable
   broth (or 1 bouillon cube)

1 Tbsp dry basil (or 10
   fresh leaves)

¼ tsp salt

¼ tsp pepper

1 tsp paprika

2 bay leaves

* See "Spices" on p.43.

MEDIUM ✖ ✖ ✖

Preparation time: 20 min.

Cooking time: 40 min.

Serves 4

Recipe:

1. Peel and mince garlic, dice onion.

2. Remove both base and tip of each carrot, and then slice into ⅛-inch circle.

3. Put olive oil in a deep saucepan and place on medium heat. Add in onions (pict. 3).

4. Cook onions for 5 minutes, stirring regularly.

5. Add ground meat (pict 4), increase heat to high and cook for 10 minutes, stirring about every minute so that meat doesn't burn.

6. Add bay leaves, paprika, Italian herbs, basil, salt, pepper and vegetable broth (pict. 5).

7. Mix well and cook for 3 minutes while mixing.

8. Lower heat to medium and add tomatoes, garlic and carrots (pict. 6).

9. Cook covered on medium heat for 15 minutes.

10. Remove bay leaves and serve.

   TIP: At step 6, you can also add a pinch of cayenne pepper to make the dish more spicy or one extra tablespoon of vegetable broth to add a more rich, salty flavor.

Ingredients

Cooking onions

Adding meat

Adding spices

Adding carrots and tomatoes

Chicken and Broccoli Rice Noodles

This is another of Cindy's favorite dishes. It makes a filling yet light meal. If you like vegetables or prefer a more crunchy meal, just double the broccoli.

The finished dish

Ingredients

Ingredients:

2 chicken breasts (1 lb)

¼ large onion, diced

2 Tbsp olive oil

4 to 6 broccoli florets
    (about 4 oz)

¼ tsp black pepper

¼ tsp salt

5 oz thin rice noodles

2 Tbsp soy sauce

1 quart of water

EASY

Preparation time: 10 min.

Cooking time: 15 min.

Serves 2

Recipe:

1. Cut chicken breast into ½-inch cubes.

2. Dice onion.

3. Cut broccoli florets into smaller pieces (pict. 2).

4. Put water in a large pot, bring to a boil on high heat and then remove from heat.

5. Place rice noodles in the hot water and let soak for 5 minutes (check package for exact time as it can vary).

6. Drain pot into colander (pict. 3) and cut noodles with scissors four or five times (to cut into approximate thirds). Set rice noodles aside.

7. Heat olive oil in a non-stick skillet on medium high heat.

8. Add onions and cook for 3 minutes, stirring.

9. Add chicken, salt and pepper, and cook for 4 minutes, regularly turning the chicken over (pict. 4).

10. Add broccoli, cover and cook for 3 minutes (pict. 5).

11. Add rice noodles (pict. 6) and soy sauce.

12. Stir well and serve.

Draining and cutting noodles

Turning chicken

Covering

Adding rice noodles

Chicken en Papillotes

Cooked in foil or parchment paper to seal in flavor and keep moist, the chicken in this dish turns out juicy and flavorful.

1

The finished dish

2

Ingredients

Ingredients:

2 chicken breasts
　　(12 to 16 oz)
1 and ½ Tbsp of rice flour
6 oz of mushrooms
2 shallots, diced
1 Tbsp olive oil
¼ tsp of salt
¼ tsp of pepper
¼ cube of vegetable bouillon

MEDIUM
Preparation time: 10 min.
Cooking time: 20 min.
Serves 2

Breading chicken

Recipe:

1. In a plate, mix and spread rice flour, salt and pepper.

2. Place chicken on plate and coat both sides with this dry mix (pict. 3).

3. Bring 4 Tbsp (¼ cup) of water to a boil on high heat in a small pot, add ¼ cube of bouillon, and mix well to make the vegetable broth. Set aside.

4. Put olive oil in a skillet on high heat and quickly sauté breaded chicken on both sides (2 minutes each side) (picts. 4 and 5). Remove from skillet and set aside.

5. Add diced shallots, mushrooms, salt and pepper to skillet and sauté for 3 minutes (pict. 6).

6. Add 2 Tbsp of vegetable broth.

7. Place each chicken breast on a piece of aluminum foil and add mushrooms on top (pict. 7).

8. Wrap each chicken breast in aluminum foil and place in the oven at 425°F for 15 minutes.

    NOTE: If you are using a thin piece of breast meat, cook for 10 minutes only.

9. Remove from the foil wrap and serve.

    SUGGESTION: You can replace chicken with turkey or a meat patty.

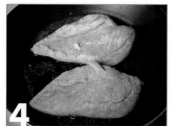

Cooking breaded chicken

Turning over chicken

Cooking mushrooms

Wrapping in foil

Chicken with Bell Peppers and Mushrooms

This easy, colorful and tasty dish provides a light, fresh meal appropriate for any occasion. Serve with rice.

The finished dish

Ingredients:

2 chicken breasts
(about 1 lb)

1 onion, sliced

½ lb of mushrooms

3 bell peppers of mixed
color, such as red
and yellow

2 Tbsp of olive oil

¼ tsp salt

¼ tsp pepper

½ tsp paprika

1 tsp dry basil or 5 or
6 leaves of fresh basil,
chopped

EASY ❌ ❌ ❌

Preparation time: 15 min.
Cooking time: 15 min.
Serves 2

Recipe:

1. Cut chicken breast into strips about a ½-inch thick by about 2-inches long.

2. Remove top of bell peppers and seeds from the center.

3. Cut bell peppers into strips about a ¼-inch thick by 1-inch long.

4. Cut onion into thin strips.

5. Cut mushrooms into 4 pieces.

6. Put olive oil in a non-stick saucepan and heat on high for 1 minute.

7. Add onion and chicken, and sprinkle paprika and pepper on top (pict. 3).

8. Stir and cook for 2 minutes.

9. Lower heat to medium high.

10. Add bell peppers, then stir and cook for 5 minutes (pict. 4).

11. Add mushrooms and basil (pict. 5), stir, and if desired, adjust seasoning to taste.

12. Cook for another 2 minutes and serve.

Ingredients

Adding onions and spices

Cooking with bell peppers

Adding mushrooms and basil

Chicken with Portobello Mushrooms

This is a sophisticated yet easy-to-make recipe that goes well with rice. Mushrooms provide an excellent source of selenium, an important nutrient in fertility.

The finished dish

Ingredients:

6 pieces of chicken
    breast tenderloins (or 2
    chicken breasts), about
    12 to 16 oz
½ large onion, diced
    (½ cup)
1 tsp rice flour
8 oz of Portobello mushrooms
2 Tbsp olive oil

¼ tsp salt
¼ tsp pepper
2 tsp basil
½ cup of water
    (for the broth)
1 Tbsp vegetable broth

EASY   ⊗
Preparation time: 10 min.
Cooking time: 25 min.
Serves 2

Ingredients

Recipe:

1. Remove stems off mushrooms and chop into ¼-inch cubes.

2. Cut chicken into small pieces (about ½ inch x ½ inch x 1 inch).

3. Pour olive oil into a non-stick skillet.

4. Stir in diced onion and cook on low heat for 5 to 10 minutes until onions are transparent (pict. 3). Stir constantly to ensure onions don't burn (they are translucent but not brown).

5. Add rice flour, vegetable broth and water. Mix well.

6. Add mushrooms (pict. 4), cover with lid and cook for 3 minutes.

7. Pull mushroom sauce to sides of cooking pan in order to leave a hole in the middle, and then add chicken to center (pict. 5).

8. Add spices on top of chicken (salt, pepper and basil) (pict. 6).

9. Cook uncovered for 5 minutes. (If using full chicken breasts instead of breast tenderloins, cook for 7 minutes.)

10. Stir chicken into mix and cook another 3 minutes.

11. Mix well and cook another 2 minutes.

12. Serve.

Cooking onions

Adding mushrooms

Adding chicken

Adding spices

Seafood

As a great source of omega-3 fatty acids, B vitamins and lean protein, seafood makes for a perfect, light main meal. Our recipes include a variety, from Hot and Spicy Prawns to a delicious, light Seafood Soup. Remember to choose seafood with low mercury levels and only consume once per week.

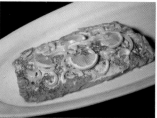

Hot and Spicy Prawns

This is a light, flavorful dish. Spicy, but not too spicy, so as not to overly tax your digestive system.

The finished dish

Ingredients

Ingredients:

1 lb prepared prawns (with tails) or peeled shrimps

8 garlic cloves, minced

2 Tbsp olive oil

¼ tsp salt

⅛ tsp pepper

¼ tsp cayenne pepper (or ⅛ tsp for a less spicy taste)

½ jalapeno

½ tsp mild pepper or paprika

EASY ⊗ ⊗ ⊗

Preparation time: 5 min.

Cooking time: 10 min.

Serves 2

Recipe:

1. Mince garlic.

2. Cut jalapeno into ¼-inch slices.

3. Cut a deep trench in each prawn (about ½ of the thickness of the prawn), from the tail to the other end. They may come already cut.

4. Spread olive oil on a non-stick skillet and place on medium high heat.

5. Add prawns, salt, pepper, garlic, cayenne pepper, mild pepper and jalapeno slices (pict. 3).

6. Stir well for 2 to 3 minutes (pict. 4), cover and cook for another 3 to 4 minutes (pict. 5).

7. Serve.

    SUGGESTIONS: You can add juice from ½ lemon at the end, stir again and cook another 1 minute. This will add a zesty taste to the dish.

    You can also make a sauce that is part of this dish by adding 1 tsp of rice flower at the end, stirring well, and then adding ½ cup of hot vegetable broth. Stir well and cook for another 2 minutes.

Adding prawns and more

Stirring mixture

Covering

Garlic Prawns

This mildly spicy dish is light and tasty. Although it seems like it uses a lot of garlic, it is well-balanced.

The finished dish

Ingredients

Ingredients:

1 lb prepared uncooked prawns (with tails on)

8 garlic cloves, minced

2 Tbsp olive oil

½ lemon juice (1 Tbsp)

¼ tsp salt

¼ tsp pepper

¼ tsp dill

EASY

Preparation time: 10 min.

Cooking time: 10 min.

Serves 2

Recipe:

1. Mince garlic.

2. Cut a deep trench in the middle of prawn, from tail to other end—about ½ of the prawn thickness. (They may come already cut.)

3. Put olive oil in a non-stick skillet and place on medium high heat.

4. Add prawns, salt, pepper and garlic (pict. 3).

5. Stir well for 5 minutes (pict. 4).

6. Add lemon juice and dill (pict. 5).

7. Stir for 2 minutes, and then serve.

SUGGESTION: You can make a sauce that mixes in with prawns by adding 1 tsp of rice flower before the lemon juice, stirring well, and then adding ½ cup hot vegetable broth. Stir well again, and then add the lemon juice.

NOTE: You can use shrimps, but make sure they are peeled, which makes them easier to eat. You can also remove the tails.

Adding ingredients

Cooking for five minutes

Adding dill and lemon juice

Steamed Fish Filet and Vegetables

This dish makes a light and healthy meal with plenty of the important omega-3 fatty acids that come with fish. Be sure to choose a fish with low mercury levels. NOTE: This recipe uses a double steamer (with two baskets). If you have a regular steamer (with one basket), you can still do this recipe. See the end of the recipe for how.

The finished dish

Ingredients

Ingredients:

1.5 lbs of fish filet (tilapia, whitefish, halibut)

½ large onion, sliced

1 lb of broccoli florets

2 zucchini

¼ tsp of salt

⅛ tsp pepper

½ tsp dill

¼ tsp dry Italian herbs*

See p.43 for "Spices."

EASY ⊗ ⊗

Preparation time: 10 min.

Cooking time: 15 min.

Serves 4

Recipe:

1. Cut onion into ⅛- to ¹⁄₁₆-inch slices.

2. Cut zucchini into ¼-inch slices.

3. Cut the broccoli into smaller pieces (as in pict. 4).

4. Place 1 inch of water in steamer pot and bring to a boil on high heat.

5. In steamer basket, lay fish filets.

6. Add onion, salt, pepper and dill (pict. 3).

7. Add basket to steamer, cover and let steam for 4 minutes (for a ¼-inch thick fish, for a ½-inch thick fish, add 3 minutes).

8. Place broccoli in second basket, add it to steamer on top of the fish, cover and continue steaming for another 4 minutes.

9. Add zucchini to broccoli basket, sprinkle with Italian herbs, and allow to steam for another 3 minutes. (picts. 5 and 6)

10. Remove steamer from heat and serve fish with vegetables, adding lemon slices for decoration and flavor.

   NOTE: If you use a single basket steamer, then first place the broccoli in basket, cover and steam for 3 minutes. Place zucchini on top of the broccoli, cover and steam for 2 more minutes. Transfer the vegetables to another pan and cover to keep warm. Now place fish in steamer basket with onion, salt, pepper and dill, cover and steam for 12 minutes. Serve.

Placing fish in basket

Broccoli in second basket

Adding zucchini

Adding Italian herbs

Baked Salmon Filet

This simple dish makes a light, healthy meal with a moist, flaky fish. Serve with basmati or wild rice and vegetables. We used sockeye salmon for this recipe.

1

The finished dish

2

Ingredients

Ingredients:

1 salmon filet (about 1 lb)

⅓ onion, sliced

½ lemon, sliced

½ tsp dill spice (dry or fresh)

⅛ tsp or less salt

⅛ tsp or less pepper

Aluminum foil

EASY

Preparation time: 10 min.

Cooking time: 30 min.

Serves 2

Recipe:

1. Preheat oven to 425°F.

2. Cut the onion into ¹⁄₁₆- to ⅛-inch slices.

3. Cut 2 round slices off the half lemon, about ⅛-inch-thick, and then cut those slices in half.

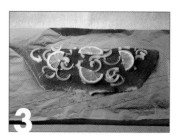

Placing fish on foil

4. Put the filet on an aluminum foil about 3 times the width of the fish (pict. 3).

5. Sprinkle salt, pepper and dill across the top.

6. Put the onion slices on top of the fish.

7. Sprinkle dill across the top.

8. Close the aluminum foil and make sure it is sealed.

9. Place in the oven and cook for 30 minutes.

10. Remove the fish from oven and open foil.

11. Using a spatula, gently separate fish from its skin (if applicable) and foil and place fish into a serving dish.

    NOTE: Fat in the fish may rise to the surface. You can scrape it off if you prefer.

Baked Fish

This is a light and juicy fish dish with many possible variations. Choose a fish with the lowest levels of mercury, such as tilapia or whitefish.

The finished dish

Ingredients

Ingredients:

1 to 1.5 lbs fish filet (such as tilapia or whitefish)

¼ tsp salt

¼ tsp pepper

¼ tsp dill

1 onion, sliced (or 3 shallots)

2 garlic cloves, minced

1 Tbsp olive oil

5 to 6 oz vegetable broth

EASY   ⊗

Preparation time: 15 min.

Cooking time: 15 min.

Serves 2

Recipe:

1. Cut onion into thin rings and mince garlic.

2. Preheat oven to 425°F.

3. Oil an oven dish and place ⅔ of onion at the bottom of dish (pict. 3).

4. Dry fish with a paper towel and lay fish on top of onion slices (pict. 4).

5. Season fish with salt, pepper and dill.

6. Spread left over onion and garlic on top of the fish.

7. Add 5 to 6 oz of vegetable broth.

8. Cook at 425°F for 15 to 20 minutes.

   NOTE: Cook for 20 to 30 minutes if using full fish (1.5 to 2 lbs of fish).

9. Serve.

   SUGGESTIONS: You can also:

   - Add 4 to 5 oz of mushrooms on top of the first layer of onion.

   - Place 2 sliced tomatoes and ½ sliced bell pepper on top of the first layer of onion and add a few black olives.

Spreading onions in dish

Placing fish on top of onions

Seafood Soup

This is a very light soup with minimal preparation.

The finished dish

Ingredients:

2 Tbsp olive oil

½ lb salmon

1 lb halibut

½ lb peeled shrimp

1 onion, diced

6 garlic cloves, minced

1 carrot

1 leek (only the white portion)

¼ tsp parsley

¼ tsp thyme

2 Tbsp vegetable broth (powder) or 2 bouillon cubes

¼ tsp each salt and pepper

EASY

Preparation time: 20 min.

Cooking time: 20 min.

Serves 4

Ingredients

Recipe:

1. Cut fish into cubes about ½- to 1-inch thick and set aside.

2. Dice onion.

3. Cut carrot and leek into small, thin slices (¼ to ⅛ inch).

Cooking onions

4. Pour olive oil into a large pot and place on medium heat.

5. Add diced onions and cook for 5 minutes, stirring frequently (pict. 3).

6. Add chopped carrot, leek, minced garlic, parsley and thyme (pict. 4).

Adding carrots and leeks

7. Cook for 5 minutes.

8. Add 2 quarts of water and vegetable broth, and bring to a boil (picts. 5 and 6).

9. Cook for 5 minutes.

10. Add fish, salt and pepper, reduce heat to medium.

Adding water

11. Cook for 5 minutes while it boils gently.

12. Serve.

> **SUGGESTION:** You can also add saffron at the time you add fish. Divide the amount by 2 if served as a side dish.

Adding vegetable broth

Soups and Salads

Soups are warm treats that nourish the body at any time of year, but especially in winter. Eat plenty of them! Our healthy, light versions include a delicious Vietnamese Chicken Noodle Soup, along with others. Because they're cold, salads are better eaten in spring and summer. They also make a refreshing alternative from the usual cooked foods and are great for picnics.

Broccoli Soup

This thick and frothy yet creamless vegetable soup is great as a quick snack by itself, or you can have it with crackers or a salad. It's easy to reheat and full of rich nutrients.

The finished dish

Ingredients:

1.5 lbs of broccoli

1 large onion

1 Tbsp dry vegetable broth (or 1 bouillon cube)

1 tsp dry Italian herbs*

1 tsp dry basil

¼ tsp celery seeds

3 garlic cloves

4 cups of water (2 for cooking and 2 to add to the blender)

½ tsp salt and ½ tsp pepper (optional)

* See "Spices" on p.43.

EASY   ⊗

Preparation time: 10 min.
Cooking time: 20 min.
Serves 5

Recipe:

1. Cut broccoli into smaller pieces (pict. 2).

2. Peel and cut onion into 4 pieces.

3. Peel and cut each garlic clove in 2, remove the germ of the garlic if applicable.

4. Put all ingredients in the pan (pict.3), including 2 cups of water.

5. Cover and bring to a boil.

6. Reduce to medium heat and let cook for 15 minutes, stirring once or twice.

7. Remove from heat and let stand for 5 to 10 minutes until mixture has cooled (pict. 4).

8. Transfer ½ the mixture to a blender and add 1 cup of water.

9. Mix at high speed for 3 to 5 minutes (pict. 5), and then place into a large bowl.

10. Do the same for the second half of the mixture.

11. Transfer all the soup mixture back to the original pan and reheat on medium for 3 minutes.

12. Serve with salt and pepper to taste.

Ingredients

Adding all ingredients

Letting soup mixture stand

Blending soup

Rice Salad

This light, colorful dish works as a main meal, side dish or appetizer. It's especially great in spring and summer.

The finished dish

Ingredients:

1 cup basmati rice
(= 4 cups cooked)

⅓ cup of salad dressing*

1 zucchini

3 oz olives

4 oz corn

¼ onion, sliced

* Use *Pierre's Vinaigrette Salad Dressing* on p.170, or use your own.

EASY ⊗ ⊗ ⊗

Preparation time: 10 min.

Cooking time: 20 min.

Serves 2 to 4

Recipe:

1. Cook rice (see recipe p.62 for *Fluffy Rice*).

2. Let rice cool in a large bowl.

3. Add salad dressing to rice and mix well.

    TIP: It is easier if you use your hands to mix.

4. Cut zucchini into small pieces.

5. Cut onion into short, thin strings.

6. Cut olives in 2 to 3 pieces, making sure the seeds have been removed.

7. Add in chopped zucchini, onion, olives and corn and mix well.

8. Serve.

    TIP: You can also add in cooked broccoli or chicken.

Ingredients

Hearty Tomato Soup

This simple soup works for summer or winter. Although fresh is better, for ease and convenience, you can substitute a can of organic diced tomatoes. It makes for great leftovers too.

The finished dish

Ingredients:

2 Tbsp olive oil

1 onion, diced

1 carrot

2 garlic cloves, minced

1 Tbsp rice flour

2 lbs tomatoes (diced)

1 quart vegetable broth

¼ tsp salt

¼ tsp pepper

2 oz soy milk

10 leaves of fresh basil
  (1 tsp dry)

EASY

Preparation time: 10 min.

Cooking time: 60 min.

Serves 4

Recipe:

1. Dice onion, mince garlic and cut carrot into small pieces.

2. Add olive oil to a large pot and sautée diced onion, garlic and carrot for 2 to 3 minutes on high heat (pict. 3).

3. Add rice flour and mix well.

4. Add tomatoes, vegetable broth (water and bouillon cube) and spices (pict. 4).

5. Reduce heat to medium, cover and simmer for 45 minutes (pict. 5).

6. Stir in soy milk.

7. Serve.

   TIP: You can add herbs before serving, like chives, cilantro or basil, both for taste and as decoration.

Ingredients

Sautéeing vegetables

Adding broth

Covering pot

Pasta Salad

This easy-to-make pasta salad provides a light, healthy meal. It's especially great in summer. Note that rice pasta doesn't taste as fresh after spending time in the refrigerator, so this dish should be eaten when made.

1

The finished dish

Ingredients:

1 lb rice pasta

4 Tbsp of salad dressing*
   (2 fl oz)

3 oz kalamata olives

5 leaves of fresh basil

¼ onion, sliced

2 tomatoes

* Use *Pierre's Vinaigrette Salad Dressing* on p.170, or use your own.

EASY ⊗ ⊗ ⊗

Preparation time: 10 min.

Cooking time: 10 min.

Serves 4

Recipe:

1. Cook the pasta according to instructions on the package.

   - Bring about 2 cups of water to a boil on high heat in a medium-size pot.

   - Add pasta and cook for the exact time it says on the package (usually 7 to 10 minutes), stirring from time to time.

Ingredients

2. Rinse the pasta in cold water by using a colander.

3. Dice tomatoes.

4. Cut onion into short strings.

5. Cut olives into 2 or 3 pieces, making sure there are no pits.

6. Add all ingredients to the pasta in a big bowl and mix well.

7. Serve.

   SUGGESTIONS: You can:

   - Add pieces of cooked broccoli or zucchini.

   - Replace olives with fresh mushrooms (baby bella or white).

   - Add cooked chicken cut in small pieces.

   TIP: Add 1 Tbsp of olive oil to the pasta when cooking to prevent it from sticking. Rice pasta has a tendency to stick more than regular wheat pasta.

Vietnamese Chicken Noodle Soup

This is a variation of the Vietnamese Pho recipe. It's flavorful, warm, comforting and so good for you.

The finished dish

Ingredients:

2 chicken breasts
  (12 to 16 oz)

¼ onion, sliced

About 10 broccoli florets
  (6 to 8 oz)

5 oz thin rice noodles

2 cubes of vegetable broth

1 jalapeno

¼ bunch of cilantro

Soy sauce (on the side)

1.5 quarts of water

10 leaves of fresh basil

1 lemon

EASY

Preparation time: 10 min.

Cooking time: 10 min.

Serves 2

Recipe:

1. Cut chicken breast into ½-inch cubes.

2. Cut onion into slices.

3. Cut broccoli into thumb-sized pieces.

4. Place water and vegetable broth in a pot and bring to a boil on high heat.

5. Add chicken and onion and let boil for 2 minutes (pict. 2).

6. Add rice noodles and cook for another 2 minutes (pict. 3).

7. Add broccoli and cook for another 1 minute (pict. 4).

8. Serve soup with soy sauce, sliced jalapeno, cilantro, basil leaves and lemon on the side (pict. 5).

NOTE: You can also add these ingredients to the soup before serving, according to taste. Add jalapeno with caution (it's hot!).

TIP: You can also add soy beans as a variation to the soup.

Adding chicken

Adding rice noodles

After adding broccoli

To serve on the side

Lentil Soup

Like other beans, lentils are rich in fiber and nutrients, with significant amounts of folate, a fertility booster. This soup is warm and hearty.

The finished dish

Ingredients

Ingredients:

1 cup of lentils

1 large onion, diced

4 garlic cloves, minced

½ tsp salt

¼ tsp pepper

1 carrot

1 leek

2 quarts of water

2 bouillon cubes

EASY

Preparation time: 20 min.

Cooking time: 30 min.

Serves 6

Recipe:

1. Dice onion and mince garlic.

2. Cut carrot and leek into small pieces.

3. Put all the ingredients in a large pot with 2 quarts of water and bring to a boil on high heat (pict. 3).

4. Lower to medium heat and cook, covered, for 30 minutes.

5. Serve.

Boiling all ingredients

Sides and Sauces

If you need a snack, make it a healthy one. This section includes favorites such as hummus and guacamole. Hummus is a popular Middle-Eastern dip made of garbanzo beans and used as an appetizer to spread on bread or crackers. The Mexican-inspired guacamole is another type of dip made from the fertility friendly avocado. Use fresh ingredients for best results. Along with these, we include a couple of French-inspired sauces which you can use on meat or rice.

Hummus

This is a great appetizer to have around for a quick snack with non-wheat crackers any time of day. The beans are also a great source of protein and fiber, and have significant amounts of folate and magnesium.

The finished dish

Ingredients:

2 15 oz cans of garbanzo beans (also called chickpeas)

The liquid content of 1 can of cooked garbanzo beans (7 oz) plus 3 oz from the second can

1 Tbsp of olive oil

2 garlic cloves

1 Tbsp of tahini paste

¼ tsp salt

Juice from 1 lemon

EASY ❌ ❌ ❌

Preparation time: 10 min.

Cooking time: 15 min.

Serves 4

Recipe:

1. Press juice out of the lemon and remove seeds.

2. Peel garlic and cut each clove into 2 parts, removing stem if needed.

3. Put garbanzo beans, 7 oz of liquid, lemon juice and all remaining ingredients into a blender (pict. 3).

4. Blend on high speed for several minutes until smooth.

5. If mixture is too thick, add slowly part of the liquid from the second can (3 oz) until mixture is smooth. You may need to help the mixer with a spoon.

   TIP: You can add an additional ¼ tsp salt or a little more lemon juice or some cayenne pepper to taste. You can also remove half of the hummus, and add cayenne pepper to the other half to serve with two different flavors.

6. Serve with baked non-wheat tortillas or crackers.

Ingredients

Blending ingredients

Guacamole

This recipe makes a great, classic appetizer—fresh and healthy. Plus, the avocado, with its healthy fats, is considered a fertility fruit. Use it as a dip or in a salad or sandwich.

The finished dish

Ingredients

Ingredients:

2 ripe avocados

1 tomato, diced (4 oz)

1 small onion, diced (2 oz)

1 lemon juice

⅛ tsp salt

⅛ tsp pepper

1/16 tsp cayenne pepper

EASY

Preparation time: 10 min.

Cooking time: 0 min.

Serves 4

Recipe:

1. Peel and cut the avocado into 4 pieces and place in a bowl (pict. 3).

2. Add diced tomatoes and onion.

3. Mash avocado into the mixture with a fork until it is well mixed (pict. 4).

4. Add salt, pepper and cayenne pepper, and mix well.

5. Add ½ tsp lemon juice and mix well with fork.

6. Serve with your favorite healthy, non-wheat crackers or chips.

Placing in bowl

Mashing with fork

Mushroom Sauce

You will be amazed that this creamy, rich, flavorful sauce has no cream, sugar or wheat. It's perfectly healthy! And it works great atop rice or meat.

The finished dish atop sliced chicken breast

Ingredients:

1 to 2 oz of dried mushrooms (cepes, morels, chanterelles; you can also use fresh mushrooms)

½ large onion, diced (or 3 shallots)

2 Tbsp olive oil

¼ tsp salt

⅛ tsp pepper

7 leaves of fresh basil, chopped

1 Tbsp rice flour

1 bouillon cube

½ cup water

1 cup soy milk

EASY ⊗ ⊗ ⊗
Preparation time: 10 min.
Cooking time: 40 min.
Serves 4

Ingredients

Recipe:

1. Soak the mushrooms in a bowl of warm water for 15 to 30 minutes. Remove mushrooms and then press them to remove additional water. Cut into small pieces or cubes. (You don't need to cut chanterelles, as they are small enough.)

2. Chop basil leaves into smaller pieces.

3. Dice onion.

Cooking onions

4. Place onions and olive oil in a non-stick pot and place on medium heat, stirring frequently (pict. 3).

5. Cook for 5 minutes.

6. Add mushrooms, salt, pepper and chopped basil, mix well (pict. 4), cover and cook for 5 minutes.

Adding mushrooms and basil

7. In a separate pot, bring 4 oz of water to a boil on high heat, add 1 bouillon cube and stir well until it dissolves to make a broth. Set aside.

8. Add rice flour in with the mushrooms and stir well (pict. 5).

Adding rice flour

9. Add broth (water and bouillon cube) in with mushrooms and stir well.

10. Add soy milk and stir well (pict. 6).

11. Cover and cook on low heat for 30 minutes, stirring every 5 to 10 minutes.

12. Serve atop rice or meat.

Adding soy milk

Healthy Béchamel Sauce

You can almost not tell there is no butter or cream in this version of the French béchamel sauce. It's light and healthy, yet still flavorful and hearty. Béchamel sauce is used as a base in many French dishes. Use on top of meat, chicken or fish.

The finished dish

Ingredients:

1 Tbsp olive oil

1 Tbsp of rice flour (or corn flour)

2 shallots, minced (or a small onion)

¼ tsp salt

¼ tsp pepper

1 Tbsp of vegetable broth powder

½ cup of soy milk

½ cup of water

EASY

Preparation time: 5 min.
Cooking time: 10 min.
Serves 2

Recipe:

1. Mince shallots.

2. Boil 1 cup of water (you will use only ½ cup of water).

3. Pour olive oil in a small non-stick pot on medium heat.

4. Add minced shallots and cook for 3 minutes, stirring regularly (pict. 3).

5. Add rice flour and stir well (pict. 4).

6. Add vegetable broth powder and stir well.

7. Add ½ cup of hot water, stir well, cook for 2 minutes and lower heat to medium (pict. 5).

8. Add soy milk (pict. 6) and stir well. When it starts to bubble, remove from heat.

SUGGESTIONS: This is the base of many sauces. You can add broken black pepper grains, curry spices and capers. You can add more shallots only or mustard (use mustard with broken mustard grains, or add after the flour if using Dijon mustard).

TIPS: If you cook a little longer after adding the soy milk, this will make the sauce thicker. Be sure to keep on low heat, though. No hard boiling.

Add a little rice flour at the end if sauce is too thin. To add rice flour, mix with 1 Tbsp of water and dilute before adding to sauce.

If you don't have powdered vegetable broth, you can dissolve 1 bouillon cube in 1 cup of water, adding in a ½ cup of this broth at step 7 in place of hot water.

Ingredients

Cooking shallots

Adding rice flour

Cooking with water added

Adding soy milk

Pierre's Vinaigrette Salad Dressing

Most off-the-shelf salad dressings have some ingredients that aren't allowed on a fertility diet. This simple, light vinaigrette tastes great and is a step up from plain oil and vinegar. It is meant to be used immediately, but will keep in the refrigerator for one week.

NOTE: This recipe calls for a small amount of yeast. Skip the yeast if you have yeast infections or endometriosis.

The finished dish

Ingredients:

¾ cup olive oil (6 fl oz)

¼ cup + 2 Tbsp vinegar
    (3 fl oz)

1 Tbsp mustard

1 tsp yeast (optional)

½ tsp salt

¼ tsp pepper

¼ tsp dry basil

¼ tsp dry Italian herbs*

1 Tbsp soy sauce

1 Tbsp soy milk

* See "Spices," on p.43.

EASY

Preparation time: 5 min.

Cooking time: 0 min.

Serves 8

Recipe:

1. Put olive oil, vinegar and mustard in a 12 oz or larger size glass jar.

2. Close lid of the jar and shake to mix. (You can also mix with a fork.)

3. Add yeast, salt, pepper and herbs. Mix well.

4. Add wheat-free soy sauce and soy milk.

5. Mix well and use.

Ingredients

NOTE: You can keep this dressing refrigerated for up to a week. Remove from the fridge 5 to 10 minutes before use to allow any oils that may have congealed to thaw. When congealed the dressing is difficult to pour, but perfectly healthy and tastes good. After it has thawed, shake and use.

Dessert

Natural sugar in the form of whole fruits and a little honey can make for a wonderful, healthy dessert. Our Juicy Fruit Salad is a medley of rich vitamins and exotic flavors that is best prepared in summer when more varieties of fruit are available. You'll find our French-inspired Crêpes Sucrées so sweet and tasty, you won't believe it contains no sugar or wheat. Although much lighter than regular crêpes, it satisfies just as deeply. You can dribble with honey for added sweetness.

Juicy Fruit Salad

This colorful fruit salad is a delicious and healthy way to satiate a sweet tooth. Eat it as breakfast or dessert. (Don't go overboard, though, and eat the whole bowl. It's natural sugar, but still sugar. Moderation is important.)

1

The finished dish

2

Ingredients

Ingredients:
2 cups of blueberries

2 cups of blackberries

12 to 15 medium-size strawberries

4 kiwis

2 bananas

1 pineapple

EASY

Preparation time: 20 min.

Cooking time: 30 min.

Serves 6

Recipe:

1. Cut outer shell of pineapple off, remove its center core, and slice what remains into small chunks (pict. 3).

2. Cut strawberries in half.

3. Peel kiwis and cut them into round, ½-inch slices (pict. 4).

4. Peel bananas and cut into ½- to ¼-inch pieces.

5. Use your hands to mix all of the above sliced fruit in a large bowl.

6. Add blackberries on top.

TIP: You can also add 2 oranges, pealed and cut into small pieces, and/or add the juice of a lemon.

Cutting pineapple

Cutting kiwi

Crêpes Sucrées

These sugar-free crêpes are intended to be used with sweet fillings, such as fruits, fruit compote or honey.

1

The finished dish

2

Ingredients

Ingredients:

1 cup of rice flour (7 oz)

6 eggs

¾ cup unsweetened
   soy milk (12 fl oz)

2 tsp olive oil

Fresh fruits (for filling)

Honey (moderate amount,
   to taste)

EASY

Preparation time: 15 min.
Cooking time: 15 min.
Serves 4 (8 crêpes)

Recipe:

1. Put rice flour in a large bowl, make a dip in center.

2. Add olive oil and soy milk into the center dip and mix well.

3. Add eggs and beat mixture until it has a uniform consistency (pict. 3).

4. Cover and let stand for 10 to 15 minutes.

5. Mix batter well with a spoon or ladle, as flour will have deposited to the bottom of the bowl.

6. Put ¼ tsp of oil in a non-stick skillet and place on medium high heat. Wait a minute or so for the pan to heat up for the first crêpe.

7. Add about ¾ cup of batter to the skillet (for a 12-inch skillet, use about ½ for a 10-inch skillet), tilting the skillet in all directions to spread the batter across its bottom surface (pict. 4).

8. Cook for 4 to 5 minutes until batter appears solid (pict. 5).

9. Flip the crêpe over and cook the other side for 3 to 4 minutes (pict. 6), and then remove from pan and set aside.

   TIP: To tell if the crêpe is ready to flip, use a spatula to see if it no longer sticks to the pan and is a little stiff. You can also peek under to see that the color has started to turn slightly brown.

(continued on next page)

Beating in eggs

Spreading batter in pan

Ready to turn over

Cooking the other side

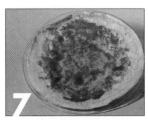

Spreading fruit compote

Rolling crêpe

NOTES: If batter has small bubbles, the heat is too high; reduce heat. Be careful not to leave the skillet on the hot burner with nothing in it (between crêpes); this will cause skillet to overheat and potentially burn crêpe. It also damages skillet.

10. Add ¼ tsp oil to skillet and repeat steps 7 to 9 until the batter is finished.

11. Serve with fruits and a dribble of honey.

SUGGESTIONS: You can also spread simple fruit compote on the crêpe (picts. 7 and 8). For fruit compote, do the following:

- Boil ¼ cup of water
- Add ½ cup of berries
- Mash with a fork, add 1 tsp of honey

You can also boil 2 Tbsp of water in the pan, add 1 Tbsp honey and 1 lemon juice (or orange) and put the crêpe in the liquid, flip it over and serve. You can also add some lemon or orange zest to boiling water (almost a crêpe suzette).

TIP: You can spread fruit compote on crêpe (as in pict. 7) and then fill with fruits before folding or rolling the crêpe. The compote helps keep the fruit from falling out.

Once made, you can keep crêpes in the refrigerators for a couple of days, wrapped in aluminum foil or Tupperware (like the pancakes).

Index

acidic, 14, 24

alcohol, 9, 11, 12, 28

alkaline, 14, 24

alkalizing effect, 15

almonds, 13, 23, 28

amino acids, 23

antioxidant, 18, 23

artificial ingredients, 14, 16

artificial sweeteners, 13, 28

avocados, 20

bacteria, 10, 15, 22, 24, 42

barley, 18, 25

beans, 4, 10, 13, 19, 23, 28, 38, 45

beverage, 10, 14, 16, 17, 24, 28

blood sugar, 9, 10, 12, 17, 18, 19, 20, 22, 23

Body Mass Index (BMI), 11, 26

bran, 14, 18

bread, 12, 14, 39, 40

caffeine, 9, 11, 12, 16, 28

cakes, 12, 40

calcium, 13, 18, 23

canned, chicken, 22

      meat, 15

      tomatoes, 5, 38, 41, 45

chamomile tea, 16, 28

cheese, 13, 23

canola oil, 20, 28, 40

carbohydrate, 10, 19, 38, 47

cereals, 12, 39, 47

cheese, 13, 23

chocolate, 11

cholesterol, 20, 22

cigarettes, 26

coffee, 11, 12, 28
cold beverages, 10
conceive, 4, 5, 6, 9, 45
conceiving, 1, 6, 11
conception, v, vi, vii, 2, 6, 9, 12
contraceptive, natural 23, 28
conversion table, 45
cookies, 12
cooking basics, 29
cooking terms, 33
couscous, 14
crackers, 14, 18, 39
creativity, 7, 29, 40
dairy, 3, 10, 13, 20, 23, 24, 38, 40, 41
decaffeinated, 12
dice, 34
digest, digestion, 9, 10, 13, 14, 16, 17, 18, 19, 21, 22, 23, 24, 28
hard-to-digest, 10, 13
dioxins, 21
durum, 14
Echinacea, 16
endocrine, 9, 13, 16, 19
endocrinologist, 1, 6
estrogen, 11, 19, 23, 24
exercise, 26, 27
fats, healthy fats, 18, 19, 20, 22, 23
monounsaturated fat, 20, 22, 23
polyunsaturated fat, 20
saturated fat, 14, 21, 21
trans fat, 14, 15, 19, 20
fiber, 17, 18, 19, 22, 23, 47
flaxseed, 20, 22, 28
flour, 14, 18, 19, 39, 40, 45
folate, 22, 23
frozen, 15, 28, 38, 41, 45
fruit juice (s), 13, 17, 18, 28

genetically modified foods, 21
heal, 3, 10
healing, 2, 11, 27
healthy fats, 18, 19, 20, 22, 23
honey, 12, 28, 47
hormones, 1, 9, 11, 13, 16, 17, 19, 21, 24
hot dogs, 22
hydrochloric acid, 24
hydrogenated oil, 19
immune, 9, 11, 12, 13, 21, 42
infertility, 6
inflammation, 14, 20, 22
ingredients, 38
insulin, 12
iodine, 22, 41
iron, 18, 21, 22, 23
isoflavones, 24
juices, fruit, 13, 17, 18, 28
        vegetable, 16, 28
        wheatgrass, 14, 17, 28
Kamut®, 28, 39, 47
labels, package 12, 13, 16, 19, 20, 38, 39
lactose, 13
LDL cholesterol, 20, 22
lifestyle factors, 11, 25
low-fat diet, vi, 19
magnesium, 17, 23
male fertility, boosting, 22, 25
maple syrup, 12, 28, 47
margarine, 20
meat, lean, 21, 29, 31, 33, 39, 62, 28
natural, 21
organic, 17, 21, 38, 28
red, 21, 28
meditation, 2, 26
mercury, 22, 28

microwave, 31
milk, 13,
    other, 13, 40
    soy, 13, 23, 24, 40
mince, 34
minerals, 17, 18, 22, 23
miscarriage, 11
monounsaturated fat, 20, 22, 23
nitrates, 15, 22
nitrites, 15, 22
non-stick, 31, 32
nourishment, 11
nuts, 20, 23, 24, 25, 28, 47
oats, 15, 39, 54
olive oil, 20, 40, 45
oils, 19, 28
omega-3 fats, fatty acid, 20, 22, 23
orange juice, 25
organic, 6, 12, 13, 17, 18, 19, 21, 23, 28, 38, 39, 40, 41, 45
oysters, 22
ovulation, 11, 16, 28
packaged, foods, 13, 14, 15, 20
meat, 21
pans, 31
partially hydrogenated oil, 15, 19
pastas, 14, 39
PCP, 15
peanuts, 23
peas, 23, 28
pH balance, 14, 24
polyunsaturated fat, 20
potassium, 23
potatoes, 18, 28
poultry, 21, 28, 34, 41
pregnant, 1, 2, 3
preservatives, 14, 15, 16, 17, 20, 21, 22, 38

processed, sugar, 9, 12, 28, 38, 47

meat, 22

progesterone, 23

prolactin, 11

protein, 14, 21, 22, 23, 47

pumpkin seeds, 22, 25

purified water, 15, 16, 24

quinoa, 14, 19, 39

raspberry leaf tea, 16, 28

raw, meat and fish, 10, 15, 21, 22, 28

  nuts, 23

reproduction or reproductive, V, VI, VII, 2, 9, 13, 16, 19, 22, 24, 26

rice, 12, 13, 14, 15, 18, 19, 28, 35, 38, 39, 40, 42, 45

sandwich meat, 15, 22

saturated fat, 14, 20, 21

saucepans, 31

sautéed, 33

seafood, 20, 22, 28, 34

seeds, 13, 22, 23, 25, 28, 39, 43

selenium, 21, 22, 25

semolina, 14

sesame, 13, 22, 25, 39

skillet, 31

smoke, smoking, 26

soda, 11

soy, 13, 14, 23, 24, 28, 39, 40

soybeans, 23

spatula, 32

spelt, 14, 19, 28, 39

sperm, V, VI, 11, 25

spices, 29, 40, 41, 42, 43

spicy, 10, 42

St. John's wort, 16

statistics, 1

steamer, 31

stevia, 12

stress or stressful, 1, 3, 9, 11, 12, 25, 26
substitutions, 5, 6, 7, 10, 29, 40
sugar, VII, 9, 12, 13, 18, 25, 28, 38, 39, 45
supplements, 2
sushi, 22
syrup, maple, 12, 28, 47
others (rice, corn), 12, 28
tabbouleh, 14
tables, 28, 35, 36, 37
tea, 11, 12, 16, 28, 42
tempeh, 23
temperature, 10, 16, 17
testosterone, 11
thyroid, 14, 24
tofu, 23, 24
tortillas, 14
toxins, 11, 25, 26
trans fats, 14, 15, 19, 20
triticale, 14
undercooked, 22
vegetables, 10, 12, 13, 15, 16, 17, 18, 19, 24, 28, 31, 33, 34, 38, 41, 42
vegetable juices, 16, 28
viruses, 24
visualizations, 2, 27
vitamins, 17, 18, 21, 22, 25, 42
walnuts, 20, 23, 28
water, bottled, 16
        drinking, 15, 16, 17, 24, 28
        purified, 15, 16, 24, 28
wheat, 3, 6, 12, 14, 15, 18, 19, 28, 29, 38, 39, 40, 45
wheatgrass juice, 14, 17
white rice, 19, 28
whole grains, 10, 12, 18, 19
whole wheat flour, 14
wine, 11